Spin off – CEO's version

Yehuda Holtzman

Spin off – CEO's version
Yehuda Holtzman

Assistance in writing chapters:

Moshe Lipsker: Changing the R&D structure

Ido Tzur: Selling the business

Editor: Ariel Rovinsky

Layout and design: Simple Story

Cover design: Lev Ari Studio

Translated by Shalom Mashbaum

simplestory
Digital Publishing

© All rights reserved to Yehuda Holtzman - 2019

Do not copy, photostat, scan, record, publish or distribute this book or parts of it, in any way whatsoever, by any electronic means, on the internet or on any other medium, without written permission of the author.

To my dear wife Zehava, for her support throughout the years,
and to my dear children Yael, Nir, and Nadav

Table of Contents

Introduction 1
The offer 8
The first month. 13
Building the lead team. 46
Business strategy – image and reality. 67
    Profitability or growth 69
    Off-the-shelf product or tailor-made
    (customized) product. 72
    One territory or global activity 75
    Patent registration - yes or no?. 82
    So what was our reality in regards to business
    strategy?. 86
Establishing vision and growth engines 92
    Strategies in regards to market, customers,
    products and our company 92
    What are our market size and share?. 94
    Who are our customers and what is
    their business model? 97
    Reviewing our products. 108

 Data Controller or Data Processor, according to GDPR 115

 What customers think of us and the NPS (Net Promoter Score) index. 122

Forming a cohesive executive team **133**

Building middle management and growth infrastructure. . . **140**

 Building an infrastructure for growth 143

 Customer Success. 144

 How do we calculate license renewal percentage? What is the correct goal?. 148

 Building an online license purchase and renewal infrastructure 153

 Online customer support. 155

Perpetual or subscription license **159**

Changing the Research & Development structure. **166**

 Assuming office 166

 Vision and strategic plan 172

 The technological revolution. 174

 The organizational change. 175

 Conclusions in retrospect 180

The brand-building plan **181**

Defining annual targets and building the annual budget **189**

 Building an annual budget. 196

The beginning-of-the-first-year crisis **202**

The unexpected assignment **206**

The sales process **211**

    Selling a business activity through an "Asset Sale"
  or a "Stock Sale" 211

    Who are the potential buyers? 216

    Finding an investment house 220

    Preparations for setting up a data room................226

Annual sales kickoff **230**

Boomerang **240**

    Earn out - a conditional-value mechanism..............240

Notifying the employees **244**

Looking back **249**

Summary **257**

Introduction

This book was written from personal experience.

After more than 20 years of management experience, both as a CEO employee and as a founding member of companies, I thought it would be difficult to find new challenges equal to those I had already undergone. But then I assumed a position which ultimately made me write this book, which summarizes a period that lasted about two years, between 2016 and 2018.

During this period, I undertook to manage the business activities of an enterprise which, in the course of the several previous years, had lost its technological and product leadership, was functioning at an operational loss, and in general seemed to have no clear future. During the two years in question, together with a skilled and focused team, this company reestablished its market leadership, began once again to produce innovative and competitive products, and regained a clear perspective for growth and profitability. These were two jam-packed and challenging years, full of interesting challenges and difficult decisions, two years which deserve to have a book written about them.

Management is a profession in and of itself, not merely an extension of some other profession. Yet, most managers do not "grow up" as managers, but enter the profession from some other position or from a different profession, ranging from a teacher who became a principal, to a programmer who advanced to run a company, to a chef who went on to run a restaurant or a restaurant chain. The essence of the management profession is very broad, and is significantly more complex than the initial job that the managers started from. It is true that the original profession, and the accumulated experience, provide understanding and knowledge regarding the professional field; however, when you reach a senior managerial position, it is not always possible to rely, long term, on these things alone.

Many managers get to learn and gain experience during their years of work on issues which may be beneficial to young managers, or to those who are seeking knowledge about certain specific cases. The case study I will describe throughout this book is indeed an excellent opportunity to learn, first-hand, about practical and real-time coping with especially complex managerial challenges, under challenging conditions.

Thus, I am presenting here an opportunity to learn from my experience, although I do not claim for a moment that all the decisions that were made proved in the end to be correct, and in the final chapter, I also indicate the mistakes that were made, in my opinion, throughout the process. But a well-known principle is that while it is good to learn from decisions that were found to be good ones, it is more important to learn from those which proved to be mistakes.

All my professional experience has been in technology companies, hi-tech, but as low-tech industries have advanced, these two areas now have much more in common than before. Therefore, managers who work in other industries will also find the experience described in these pages of great interest.

The book deals with a case of a spin-off, that is, removing a business activity from an active company which has a number of different business units which are so different from one another that the disadvantage of having all of them under one umbrella is greater than the advantage, and therefore a spin-off takes place.

A spin-off enables every business activity to focus only on itself, and at the end of the process, one or both activities are usually sold. This was the second time I became involved in a spin-off. The first time was in 1998, and actually dealt with establishing a company from scratch, with a basic technological capability, and an initial investment of $2 million.

This time the challenge was different, although the basic story is that of a progression of events that is quite common in companies that exist for several years. We are speaking of a company which was founded in 1999, and operated in a field called the Mobile Life Cycle, MLC. The company developed a product that backs up data which are stored in a cellphone, or transfers them to a new or alternate cellphone.

During the first years of its operations, the company concentrated only on this activity, but in 2007, it expanded its business activity to another field, digital forensics.

In order to try to preserve both activities, the organization was divided into two business divisions; each division had its own designated employees, such as salespeople, product management employees, and developers, while common corporate functions, such as finance, human resources, and IT, remained shared. The company continued to operate in this way for a number of years, during which time, called the "split period," the MLC division even launched a new product line, in the field of diagnosis of cellphone malfunctions.

The field of digital forensics developed rapidly, so that only a few years after it was launched, it became the company's main growth engine. As time passed, the focus of senior management concentrated on the field of digital forensics, which led the company both in revenue and profitability, and so naturally the company's original area of activity, MLC, entered into a state of responsive, rather than strategic management. Of course, this situation damaged the status of the MLC division among customers, and was also reflected in its business results. Market growth precipitated the entry of new competitors, which gained market share and leadership at the expense of the MLC division, resulting in an operational loss during a certain period.

The company's senior management identified this dynamic situation, and decided to split the business activities, through the establishment of a separate company for the MLC activity. In this way, a separate management team could be assigned to the new company, which would give the MLC activity its full attention and get it back on the track of growth and profitability. At this point in time, I was approached with an offer to head the new company, and carry out this mission.

At that time, the MLC activity numbered about 140 employees, while still a significant part of the two business activities was being shared, which in itself was a challenge to me in terms of executing the spin-off.

The book begins with an examination of my considerations for accepting the job, and immediately moves on to survey my entry into the job and my immediate dive into the details, almost without coming up for air, because there was no time to do so. I had to become intimately familiar with the condition of the business as soon as possible, to identify its weaknesses and strengths, to inspect the existing team across its multiple offices around the world, to build a new team as needed which would be able to formulate and execute a new business strategy, to accompany and inspect the progress towards the set goals, and to make difficult decisions on a daily basis. In addition, in the last third of this job, all this was done in parallel with (partly confidential) negotiations for the sale of the MLC business, which also added emotional difficulty to the operational complexity.

In some chapters, we dive into high-resolution details, in

order to clarify, as much as possible, the challenges we faced, and to enable the reader to understand some of the decisions we made, especially with regard to how we implemented business analysis, identified market trends, and evaluated product value as perceived by potential customers. Detailed examples and explanations of many issues are also provided, such as what motivates some customers to pay a high price for a particular product, and on the other hand, what drives other customers who are not ready to pay for the same product.

On the other hand, some issues are treated in less detail, due to information confidentiality, but this will not detract from the reader's ability to understand our information analysis process, and the actions which we took in the course of the business rehabilitation, and up to the sale of the business.

There is no need to mention that after food and oxygen, cellphones are the next most important thing to human beings. This book presents an analysis of different business models in this field, so that in addition to a description of business aspects and analyses of our MLC products, an explanation of the retail world for the sale/purchase of cellphones is presented, as well as one of repairs and insurance of these devices.

I also asked some members of the company senior management to add their viewpoint in regards to certain subjects. I had two motivations for this:

- It enabled me to give as broad a perspective as possible, from many different angles, regarding processes or decisions that were critical in determining the future of the company.
- It enabled me to present the different sensitivities to certain subjects of different members of management, each one with different responsibilities.

Wherever the information in this book was written by another member of the company's senior management, details about them were noted.

This book deals with a single case in a particular field, and naturally will be very interesting to any person involved in setting up a separate business activity within an existing business, or considering performing a spin-off. But precisely the uniqueness of the story told here, which requires a very detailed elaboration of certain challenges, thought processes and aspects of management, makes the book interesting and relevant to any young high-tech manager, and indeed for anyone interested in management in the broad sense of the word.

There are many approaches to management, similar to training in sports. In basketball, for example, there are coaches who advocate the crucial importance of defense, and accordingly, players will be chosen according to their defensive ability, while other coaches will concentrate on offense. Some coaches believe in similar playing time for all players, and there are those that will allow a small number of players, only the outstanding ones, to play a long time in each game. Some prefer fast breaks, and some prefer organized offensive plays; some prefer shots only from inside the three-point line, while some are in favor of three-point shots. It is important to emphasize that there is no "right" or "wrong" approach; what counts is the end result – where the team finds itself in the league at the end of the year, compared with the target it set for itself.

Similarly, our management approach will define the managers we recruit. Managers with different approaches will recruit subordinate managers with a similar or complementary approach, or those who can make adjustments to the manager's approach. Also, something that happens not infrequently in group sports, where a certain player may not succeed on one team but is very successful on another team, also happens in the workplace. In the end, everything starts and ends with people - how they fit into the designated DNA of the organization, and the ability of the manager to identify each one's potential, and to build the right team for the right task.

The offer

When we are looking for a job, or when someone approaches us with a job offer, each of us will consider the offer's value differently. Moreover, an offer that would be considered attractive at a particular point in time in our lives may become irrelevant several years later, and vice versa.

When we consider the value of a job opportunity, first we must define the parameters that are important to us, and then define each parameter's relative weight. However, the parameters can change over time, according to our personal, financial and professional situation, and it is also very possible that at different times, certain parameters will have different weights.

Moreover, even if we take two people of the same age who are on the same professional track, it is very possible that they will define different parameters, and/or assign different weights to the same parameters.

The variables that usually interest us in a job offer include:

- **How interesting is the job** – to what extent can I realize myself?
- **Monthly salary.**
- **Benefits and incentives** - insurance, bonuses, options/shares, meals, training seminars.
- **Organizational culture** and its appropriateness to my values and perceptions.

- **The human environment** - the people I am supposed to work with.
- **Learning and development.**
- **Job security.**
- **Work comfort** - work environment, travel distance, flexibility in hours, willingness to working from home, and more.
- **Position and status** - (expert, manager, director, member of senior management) and many more parameters that each person adds and takes into account before making a decision.

When we are making a decision about a job offer, it is very important to also look at the process from the opposite angle - that is, to examine how well we fit the job. The same evaluation process that we perform for the job, we should perform for our fitness to the position offered as well.

It is important for everyone to know what their own strengths and weaknesses are, and if they have doubts, not to be embarrassed to initiate, confidentially, a kind of 360° inquiry, that is, to ask for an evaluation of themselves from:

- Former managers, and other managers in parallel positions with whom they had contact.
- Colleagues in the same department, or other employees with whom they interfaced.
- Employees they managed.

Over the years, I got to work with hundreds, if not thousands, of people, and getting a perspective on my strengths and weaknesses from them never hurt.

At the beginning of my career as a manager, I sold equipment worth tens of millions of dollars, and I did this successfully. However, of the dozens of salespeople I recruited further down the road, I recognized that the best of them, the ones who knew how to manage the customer during the challenging moments of the sale stage, were better than I was in this area.

I experienced a similar phenomenon a little earlier. After completing my engineering studies, I worked in R&D for eight years, and although I thought I was really good, after ongoing work with quite a few other engineers, I realized that there are much better engineers than I am. Over time, I learned to identify where my strengths lie: in the line which connects the identification of the business need and the appropriate technology to the solution, and the ability to manage people, to get more out of them than they had produced so far, both as individuals and as a group.

The message: It is important to identify your strengths, to know in what situations you stand out, and to include this information in the set of parameters to check when you look at your future path.

As for myself, at the time, in the context of what I was looking for, I was interested in only one thing – a challenge. I was not looking for a calm and stable place; I was looking for an opportunity to take a certain business activity, and make a significant positive change in it over a short period of time.

Over the course of two months, I received three relevant initial proposals:

The first was from a new company with very interesting technology: algorithm-based software for business applications. But since I got negative references about the owners, that was sufficient for me to reject the offer.

The second job offer was from a company with close to 80 employees which was growing at a moderate pace, but since I knew their market, I didn't think that with the budget at the company's disposal, it would be possible to make significant change, and bring about major growth, in the course of two or three years.

I received the third offer after I had decided that I would not move forward on the other two. This time, the offer came from a company with more than 500 employees, which was composed of two business divisions, one of which was on a steady rise in its business activity, with impressive performance, and a second one which had been declining steadily for several years, both in business volume and market share in different global locations, and was operating at a financial loss.

This division operated in the MLC (Mobile Life Cycle) market, and the goal of the company's owners and senior executives was to separate the two divisions completely, and then make the changes necessary to put the MLC division back on the track of profitability and growth.

Since the two areas the company was engaged in had almost nothing in common, the goal was not only to separate them administratively and logistically, but eventually to create a separate legal entity.

[It is important to note that in general, in order to bring a business activity to profitability, especially in large companies with a number of different business divisions, there is usually no real need to create a separate legal entity in order to perform a business division. The motivation to spin-off a division into a separate legal entity usually comes from a desire to change the ownership structure, such as introducing a new investor, a stock issue, or a sale.]

All parameters in this case showed positive indications:

1. **Business challenge** - Take a medium-sized business that is active worldwide, and significantly change its activity on most levels, in order to generate growth and profitability.

2. **New market** - Although I knew the cellular market well, my knowledge was mainly in network planning and infrastructure, rather than on the retail side, and it is always interesting and challenging to enter a new market.
3. **Economic basis** - An established company that has the financial ability to invest in order to make a change.
4. **Mutual aspirations** - Diverse parties, all of whom support the change. That is, when I checked the various parties who had an impact on the decision about the new path of the MLC division, I determined that everyone felt that it's worthwhile to go in the direction chosen.

I was not looking to tie myself down to a long-term commitment in any way. Not only was it clear to me that I wouldn't know what the real condition of the business was until the end of the first months, but, more importantly to me, I had to make sure I would be getting extensive, unrestrained room for action.

The process of being accepted was very short. Our contract was signed within two weeks, but due to happy personal circumstances, I put off starting the work for two months, until early June, 2016.

During the interim period, I was mostly interested in one thing - discovering the real condition of the business activity I took upon myself. Spoiler: At least there is one thing I can already reveal: in terms of the challenge – this job met my expectations!

The first month

As I started working for the company, my goal was to gather as much information as possible in the shortest time, to understand the real current situation, and to gain initial insights into the changes which would be needed to put the organization back on the track of growth and profitability.

At the same time, we must understand the employees' concerns about the process of splitting the business activities into two companies. For them, doing so means leaving a very stable place and marching into the unknown.

In practical terms, this situation was expressed in 14 hours of work in the office per day, holding six daily meetings in order to meet "one on one" with at least 80% of employees, in order to both listen and learn, and at the same time say enough to create interest and hope.

I was given no more than 48 hours of grace, and already on the second day on the job, I was asked to join important discussions that all dealt with the same subject - complaints from customers that we do not fulfill what was promised them. I felt like someone put in front of a crumbling dam, in which every moment another hole opens up. I do not remember a single customer about whom I could say they were pleased. There were not only complaints about our failure to keep promises, but also complaints that we are not innovative enough in products and/or technologies.

We will return to the customers' findings later, and focus first on the personal meetings. Every two or three days, I focused on a different department, with the intention of hearing from a number of people from the same department each time. There were immediate diagnoses, and I felt comfortable in already drawing preliminary conclusions after the first two weeks.

Meetings with employees in the HQ

Sales

Let's start with the **sales group**. Here the challenge was complex, because it is difficult to have deep familiarity conversations when you do not meet face to face, and in the original structure, only three salespeople were in the HQ, and the rest were in different places around the world. At the initial stage, I met with the local three, and in addition, I invited the VP sales manager who led the activity in North America, and also the one who managed South America, to the HQ. Only after the first three weeks did I go abroad to meet the employees in the various offices overseas.

Among the three HQ-based employees was Alon Schnitzer, who at the time ran the European operations, except for the DACH countries (Germany, Austria, and Switzerland). He pointed out that we have four main challenges:

1. Our product and technological leadership have been steadily eroding for years, allowing new players to enter the field and take important market shares away from us. We are not launching innovative capabilities or new products, and concentrate mainly on additions, which are kind of "evolution but not revolution." The basic problem is – there is no vision, the direction the company is going in is not clear.

2. We do not keep promises. We commit ourselves to developments for a number of Tier1 customers, but we don't meet the deadlines, or in the end, we simply don't perform what we promised we would.

3. Response time to basic customer requirements, even on the elementary level of text change or basic visibility, is measured in months, which is completely unacceptable.

4. User interface and user experience (UI/UX) are obsolete, and far from what customers expect to see.

I did not receive a clear answer to my question about license renewal by long-term customers. We will get back to this important issue later.

Similar messages came from meetings with other salespeople in our HQ:

- As time passes, our lack of progress in terms of technological and product innovation reduces our ability to compete.
- Our response to customer demands includes a lot of promises, but little is actually performed, and even that later than necessary.

Quality Assurance

After meetings with the salespeople, I focused on the quality assurance (QA) team. It was important for me to hear the team leaders in parallel with the meetings I had begun to participate in that focused on customer complaints. The message that came from the conversations with the quality team employees was consistent:

1. **Defective code infrastructure** – this was the most serious problem. Everyone noted that every time you add a new feature or functionality to the product, you create

problems with the existing functionality, so that in practice, the regression tests (checking the effect of adding a new function on the original product performance) accounted for most of the testing time, consuming most of the development time to neutralizing regression problems. When this happens time after time, all indications are that the architecture of the code infrastructure is poor. This is a basic problem whose source is the quality of the infrastructure, a problem that has been expanding and deepening for several years now.

2. **Insufficient development quality** – another issue that arose is that often, the QA team received new features for testing that were not ready for QA tests; sometimes even minimal tests weren't performed during development, but since the time allotted for development was over, the changes were sent to QA for review regardless of their level of readiness. When you connect this problem to the salespeople's complaints about the waiting time of months for changes, this indicates a possible problem with the development methodology. We will elaborate later on this topic.

3. **Automated testing** – When I asked about automated tests, the answer was "almost nonexistent,"; this was again attributed to regression failures, that consume the vast majority of testing time and are unpredictable and therefore cannot be automated.

After the QA (software testing and product quality assurance) interviews, I interviewed a large number of development personnel. Here is the place to take a short break and talk about software development methodologies. I will relate to two main methods – linear methodologies and agile methodologies:

Linear methodologies – There are several methods in this category, the main one being:

__Waterfall__ is an established methodology for the development of software systems. In this model, software development is carried out in a systematic and logical process composed of well-defined stages that must not be skipped over. The steps are executed in series, one at a time, and at each stage, there is only one main task. There is a great deal of emphasis placed on the collection and analysis of all the requirements before the start of development, and there is no backtracking in the process after a certain stage has ended.

(Wikipedia)

Agile methodologies – methodologies built from repetitive operations which have been adapted for software development by small teams, with an emphasis on efficiency, agility, and quality. Agile methodologies structurally include changes in the software specifications, and are built to respond to them quickly. Compared to linear methodologies, the time between releasing different software versions is much shorter. The main agile methodology as of that time was SCRUM.

***SCRUM** – is an agile methodology for managing software development projects; the basic emphasis of the method is on teams that direct themselves, as well as an experimental (empirical) cyclical process that is not defined in advance. The term SCRUM originates from the game rugby; there the term describes the way in which the game starts again after the ball goes out of the field.*

The technique of "re-starting" is one of the foundation stones of the method – a SCRUM project restarts the development process every few weeks (let's say a month); i.e., once a month, functioning software is provided to the users, and their comments, as well as new requirements, are implemented in subsequent development cycles.

Wikipedia

Back to meetings with developers

In fact, the R&D department included two separate groups – research, and development. The development group numbered 50 people (separately from the QA group of approximately 30 people), and the research team, a small number of researchers.

I met with the R&D Vice President, with the group managers, and with many developers.

Their statements were very different, and focused on different issues, depending on their role. The R&D VP referred mainly to the inability of the product managers to set a forward-looking roadmap. There was no horizon and clarity as to where the company was going, and what future products were going to be.

The claims of the development group managers focused on four main issues:

1. **Lack of understanding of where the company is going** – continuing what the R&D VP said, they, too, felt that there was no clear horizon. The company had been producing the same functionality for several years, while quite a few competitors have been added in recent years. What is our vision?

2. **Products that do not reflect market needs** – new products or functions which must be developed were defectively and incompletely defined by the product managers, so that in many cases, the developed result did not reflect the market needs.

3. **Development without adequate architectural definition** – Various products were being developed on different platforms without the definition of an architect or of system engineers.
4. Lack in structured **Infrastructure and code** – the architecture and code infrastructure of the core platform were in bad shape, and insufficient time had been allocated to improve them. The current situation caused inefficiency each time a new functionality was added.

When I drilled deeper into the details, I realized that the code was written in such a way so that even the smallest change takes weeks to make, mainly because the basic code is built with multiple dependencies between the different layers, resulting in regression problems. That is, most of the development time is not required for adding this or that patch, but for testing to ensure that existing functionality is not compromised.

The research team, which included a small number of researchers, had a critical role in the development of unique and differentiating technologies, which set our products apart from those of our competition. I will elaborate on this later. In my opinion, achieving a substantial technological advantage, which translates into substantive quality/performance differentiations between competing products, enabling a company's products to stand out, is the basis for leading a company to success. Of course, achieving a technological advantage is an unending goal, since, after all, it has to be continuously rebuilt.

The researchers raised several arguments:

1. **The organization does not understand what research work is** – unlike writing code, for which it is possible, based on experience, to estimate the time needed to perform a task, in research work, this is almost impossible. There is a problem that needs to be solved, and finding a solution

takes time. It can take a week, months, and it also may not take place at all.

2. **No consistent priority for the research team** – Priorities in which topics must be researched varies every few days, which prevents any work from ending.

3. **Lack of adequate research infrastructure** – no time and tools were provided to build strong research infrastructures that improve work efficiency.

4. **Lack of understanding of the importance of Big Data** – the supervisors did not understand the need to build infrastructure and the ability to manage and analyze a large amount of data – Big Data. The company "touched" millions of phones a year. In addition, every new phone developed by the leading manufacturers was obtained by the company for examination and research. The bottom line is that the company has – or should have – an "infinite" database from which much could be derived. For example, the company can know how many times a particular phone has fallen in the course of its life, and what damage was done to it each time. If this information is processed skillfully, it is worth a great deal – to phone manufacturers, to insurance companies, and to many other parties – but an appropriate infrastructure must be built for this purpose, and this was not done.

Product management

The next group I met was **product management and business development**. In my opinion, the role of product management is the most important one in the organization. The scope of the role will vary among different companies depending on their size, the life cycle of the product, the market in which they operate, and many other parameters, but again – this is a role that should include managing the entire product life cycle, which includes:

- **Define the problem and identifying opportunities.**
- **Calculating the investment required to enter the market.**
- **Mapping competitors.**
- **Setting prices and profitability.**
- **Defining new products.**
- **Estimating the expected product life/fixed investment level needed to maintain market position.**
- **Planning market entry strategy.**
- **Calculating profit and loss (P&L) by product.**

Of course, this list of requirements makes it difficult to find suitable people. In general, I see the product manager as a kind of mini-CEO, since the product managers touch and have a direct impact on each function in the organization. That is why compensation of product managers should be directly related to meeting the business activity objectives of the company, including sales and profitability of the product.

In practice, there was a very large gap between what was to be expected of the product managers and what was carried out. In addition, there were product managers who did not see all the tasks which I mentioned as tasks that they should be responsible for. How does one deal with such a situation? That will be explained later on.

Because I will not return later in the book to discuss what product manager should be responsible for; I'll use this opportunity to expand here on some of the topics which were defined as headers only:

1. **Defining the problem and identifying opportunities** – You can divide opportunity identification into two types:

    ♦ Identification of a new feature that originates from the product manager themselves and <u>not</u> from the salespeople

    ♦ Requests from customers or salespeople. In this case, there are two options:

    Option 1 – The product manager evaluates and decides not to add this feature.

    Option 2 – The product manager identifies the feature as an important need which should be added to the product.

    At this point in time, under option 2, it must be understood that the source of the request for the feature is the customer, and that, in <u>most cases</u>, the need for the feature was transferred simultaneously to competitors, or that the customer has heard of this capability from competitors (ours or theirs), and they want to know if we can add it. In practice, no matter how we turn this around, there is a very high probability that our competitors already have the particular capability being requested, or are working on a solution.

    In this case, the manager has to decide how they are to prioritize this request for a feature – this is not a simple process, because if we give priority to a new request, that means postponing another request that we have already committed ourselves to.

2. **Calculating the investment required to enter the market** – what is the cost of the project, in terms of money and time, which includes the entire cycle from product definition through research and development, product launch, and all that is related to the operation and sales of the product until we reach the breakeven point, in which the revenue from the product equals its operational expenses?

    Calculating the cost will allow the company to understand:

- Is this a project that the company can support?
- What is the target for return on investment, from a time and risk perspective?
- Investment alternatives – that is, given the time and budget required, can they be used better elsewhere?

3. **Mapping competitors**

   The market by its nature is characterized by competition. Accurate mapping of competitors is vital to coping successfully with the challenge of competition.

   Who is considered a competitor?

   - **Direct competitors** – providing the same types of products or services.
   - **Competitors who provide alternative products/services** – for example, to a company which is considering entering the field of drones for shipping, taxis and missions in scooters should be considered competitors, because they indeed provide the same service, although we are not speaking of another company that produces drones.
   - **Potential future competitors** – There are several types of companies which it is important to catalog as potential competitors, including:
     - Companies with different products that serve the same customer market, and are considering expanding into new products, who have the capabilities required for expansion to a competing product line.
     - Companies that have a similar product, but focus on a different geographical area or a different market. Their expanding to additional markets will make them competitors.

Analysis of competition characteristics

- Number of competitors: Is this a market full of competitors with similar market share, or is it one controlled by a small number of players? A market which is dominated by a small number of players is much more difficult to penetrate than a distributed market that has many small players.

- The intensity of the competition: is it aggressive, or is it moderate and characterized by cooperation between competitors?

Analysis of competitors

The mapping and analysis of competitors will include details such as:

- Seniority in the market.
- Financial strength: profitability, working capital, investors.
- Target markets: both vertical and geographic.
- Sales volumes and trends in recent years.
- The company's market share.
- Unique technological capabilities, patents.
- Pricing strategy.
- Marketing strategies and market penetration: salespeople, sales channels, collaboration, online, OEM.
- Company and product positioning.
- Detailed comparison of products.

Understanding the competitive landscape, beyond formulating parameters such as product's pricing, sales & marketing strategy, will lead to the definition of a target for positioning the company and its products in reference to each of its important competitors.

In addition, it will be possible to mark the main competitor or competitors in relation to the target market segment, and to set targets for market share and sales in a given period of time.

4. **Setting prices and profitability** – what price we can charge for the product and in accordance with this, what will the profitability be?

   According to the existing competition (direct or indirect), what will be the range of prices for the type of product or service we provide? We must set the price of the product in accordance with the uniqueness of our solution, as compared to other solutions within our target market.

   An analysis of price elasticity is important; that is, will changing the price result in a change in the number of customers, and if so, what is the expected change?

   Very simplistically – if we can build a matrix of quantity versus price, we can estimate the income, the profit, and the profitability level for the price that was set.

5. **Estimating product life/fixed investment level needed to maintain market position** As an example: Most products based on software, will require a level of modification and maintenance (bug fixes, new platform adaptations, adaptation to new hardware infrastructures, updating or adding features, etc.). It is important to build a model that will predict the investment required to maintain the product throughout its life.

Marketing

The next team I met with was **marketing**: it was a one-man team, Jade Kahn, originally an Australian, who operated subcontractors and was assisted by the digital forensic division in managing the marketing activity, which was very limited.

It was clear that we need to build everything from scratch, because we were missing basic functionalities:

1. Because there was one website for both businesses, including one engine for marketing messaging, it was very difficult to build a brand for MLC. Actually, the first thing that we needed was a plan for creating our brand.

2. At the same time, all customer orders went through salespeople, whether external or internal (inside sales). A single license renewal purchase order in the sum of several hundred dollars would pass through a whole sales route, a fact which by definition produces a non-profitable result. The need to add a sales engine for single renewals or purchase of just one product on a marketing platform (we will elaborate on this issue later) was obvious.

3. Also lacking was a broad and controlled process of lead generation. Lead generation is a systematic process of creating potential customers' interest in the company and in its products, as a first stage in making them into customers. Marketing activity of lead generation includes a combination of phone calls to customers, exhibitions, events, internet activity, social networking, e-mail, traditional direct mailing, webinars and more.

    In lead generation, there is a great deal of emphasis on measuring activities effectiveness using supporting software, with the goal of adopting them in order to build an orderly process.

4. Analytical information on the market was missing. There was no function in the organization responsible to ensure receipt of timely and up-to-date market information, so that on the one hand, decisions could be made, and, on the other hand, decisions that had already been made could be examined in view of new information which was received.

With regard to market research, here we must warn against generalization, that is, the company should avoid performing a single, overall global market analysis; the accuracy of such an analysis is doubtful. In many of the cases I have encountered in the past, different geographic markets require different market analyses, due to:

- Local regulations.
- Different cost structure, different taxation.
- Local competition.

It is always advisable to request different market analyses for different territories, which will include:

- Calculation of Total Available Market (TAM).
- Calculation of the Serviceable Addressable Market (SAM).
- Market Growth/reduction rate for the most recent three to five years.
- Competitors.
- Leading players' market share.

Even if market research has been done that provided important information, it is not a substitute for almost real-time information on many topics that we will relate to later on.

Summary of meetings with employees in the HQ

I met with most of the employees, and was favorably impressed. I met employees who felt, on the one hand, that they had been cut off from the stable base of the main ship and were on a raft whose direction is not clear, and on the other hand, they had a strong and genuine desire to contribute as much as would be needed to lead to the success of a business activity that had become independent.

The meetings were businesslike; the issues were presented and discussed very candidly.

The employees were not pointing accusing fingers, they just wanted to change things that needed changing.

A summary of the main topics I wrote down for myself included:

- Frustration and concern about the erosion of the product and the technological advantage that the company had some years ago.
- A lack of trust between development groups and product management.
- A complex code infrastructure that made adding capabilities and fixing problems difficult.
- A research team, that is supposed to be the spearhead in differentiation, setting our product apart, which was not operated properly.
- There was a need to build a brand and establish a new marketing infrastructure.

Regarding the issue of license renewal – I was troubled by the fact that I could not find any data from which conclusions could be drawn. The licenses that the company sold so far were for the most part Perpetual Licenses. The company offered an annual (or three-year) support package, which included software updates, bug fixes, and most importantly, up-to-date support for new phones, but if the support package is not renewed, the utilization and the level of use of our products will be reduced, which will damage the purchase of new products. This subject was disturbing and demanded a deep investigation.

Meetings with employees abroad

During the fourth and fifth week on the job, I visited the company's various offices around the world: Germany, Singapore, Japan, the US, and Brazil.

Before we go over the summaries of the meetings, it is important to describe in greater detail the company's products, who were our customers, and what was their motive for purchasing our products.

We had two main products, both sold as application layers on top of our hardware platform.

The first and foremost product was Content Transfer, whose purpose was to transfer the contents of a phone to another phone, from any type of phone to any type of phone.

The second product, Diagnostics, was relatively new and used by a small number of customers, mainly in Europe, whose purpose is to find out if there is a problem with the cellphone. If there is a software problem: a problematic app, bad phone settings, or a virus – the product is designed to solve the problem.

Our products were sold mainly to retail chains of cellular operators in North America and Europe. The operators sell phones through these chains, and beyond the profit they make on the sale of handsets and various accessories, they take advantage of this sale to link the user to their cellular network, where profitability from the network usage should be high; usually, the customer will pay for the phone he has purchased in installments, as part of the bill for using the network. This payment is made at the end of the month, after monthly use (postpaid).

Germany

The EMEA office (Europe - Middle East – Africa), was in Germany, where the sales director to the DACH countries (Germany, Austria, and Switzerland) was based. In addition to two salesmen and a sales engineer, our presence in Germany included a function which was responsible for the sales operation, and a technical support employee who was part of the company's global support team.

This division between the European countries – between the team that was in Germany and managed the DACH countries, and those who were in the HQ and managed the rest of the countries on the continent – was made for historical reasons, mainly to support the business activity of the digital forensics division, but there was nothing in it that made sense to us. When serving global customers who have representation in all the leading countries, it is very difficult to support them when there is no single leading manager.

As far as the German office was concerned, 2016 was on its way to being a bad year, and the outlook for the future did not seem exciting. During meetings with employees, I was mostly in a mode of listening to the issues they raised, and I raised questions so that together we could sharpen the essence of the challenges. Beyond the issue of technology and product stagnation and lack of clarity as to where the business operations headed, we quickly identified the significant points that need to be addressed in depth:

1. **The trend of online purchases** – our current products are sold in retail stores which sell cellphones. Germany is the country in which the percentage of purchasers of phones through the internet, and not in stores, is the highest among European countries and America, a fact that in practice reduces the use of our current product (we will expand regarding our products later on, so that things will become clearer). Actually, in Germany, more people buy through the internet in comparison to stores, and this trend will continue, so that we can already

expect a decline in the size of our market if we do not release a suitable product.

2. **Customer service failures** – There were serious complaints from large customers about the quality of our customer service in German, especially regarding service availability and length of time getting answers. Here, too, the problem was immediately apparent – when one German-speaking technical support employee is supposed to provide a solution for customers who are active 10 hours a day, seven days a week, and from the outset, our service is available only five days a week, this is not a satisfactory service situation.

3. **Updates which take hours** – There were customer complaints about software update time. The quality of the Internet network in the stores, both wired and wireless, is low, which leads to very long times (hours) for downloads and software updates to our current product, which is based on unique hardware.

4. **Competition** – Another important troubling point was the activity of a competitor who has been in the market for several years and developed a software-only system, which began to eat into our market share in Europe. Our competitor's main advantage was their price, because they did not need dedicated hardware. It's not that everything is rosy for the competitor, but for individual stores or small chain stores that are able to connect multiple applications on a computer without many IT approvals, the competitor's cheaper solution was an advantage.

I'll explain this point in detail: the point of payment in the stores is a computer for all intents and purposes, which can be used to take advantage of additional applications, such as one that offers the functionality we offer, that is, the ability to transfer all information from one phone to another. If the competitor software can be installed on the computer at the point of payment, thus saving significant expenses. If a high-quality computer for a store costs $700, and if the network has 1,000 stores, they can save $700,000, and even beyond that, they save on the operational expenses of maintaining 1,000 additional computers, something that sounds simple, but in practice is a big headache and involves considerable cost. In practice, mainly in medium and large networks, IT (Information Technology) departments do not allow adding apps to payment points due to concern about introducing security loopholes that will allow information theft. Still, even in a situation in which another dedicated computer is used, the competition has an advantage over using a non-standard hardware platform due to lower operating expenses.

At the end of the visit to Germany, I emphasized to the employees that in three months' time, we would present a business plan that will contain a response to the main challenges mentioned.

From Munich, I went on to Singapore.

Singapore

In the past, I worked for many years with Singapore companies, within the framework of the previous companies I managed. We had customers in Singapore and local distributors covering also neighboring countries, especially Malaysia and Indonesia.

In this case, Singapore was our company's business center in Asia (excluding Japan), including Australia and New Zealand.

I spent two days in Singapore. One intensive day with three staff members, and another day with businessmen I had been in contact with for years in order to get their perspective.

There was an interesting cross-checking between the various

meetings. When we went over our business performance so far, a number of things were conspicuous:

- A large accumulation of opportunities that for many months have not been realized.

- The accumulation of opportunities was geographically dispersed. I did not find a concentration in any one country, but in a very broad deployment across 10 countries, each of which with a very limited number of opportunities.

- Very poor forecast of income by the end of the year.

The deeper we discussed the business models of our potential customers, even to the point of flow of money between consumers – the stores – the operators – phone manufacturers, one point arose that we all agreed upon regarding its decisive weight in relation to the type of product that may be promoted, and even more importantly, about the payment model that can be promoted in Asia.

I will specify: Cellular operators prefer to create some commitment on the part of the customer. The commitment is reflected in the contract signed between the user and the operator, which specifies the service received by the customer (usually call minutes, unlimited SMS messages, and a limited amount of data traffic, usually a few gigabytes), as well as how much money the operator will receive at the end of each month for using the cellular network. In order to strengthen the commitment of the user to the operator, most operators will offer the customer the opportunity to purchase the cellular phone through them, under good financial conditions, which usually include paying in installments for the new phone, as part of the customer's bill for using the network at the end of each month. Through this process, the cellular network operators increase the chance of steady income from using the cellular network in the following years, enabling them to have accurate future financial planning.

Our products have helped stores that sell phones, including stores of the cellular operators themselves, to significantly shorten the time needed to transfer all data to the new phone, thus contributing to improving service to their customers.

In order to gain perspective, from information that exists on the internet: the four leading mobile phone sellers in the US in 2017 were all cellular operators, because of what I explained earlier – the payment for the phone is linked to the payments for the use of the cellular network (which generates the most profitable revenue), which are thus almost guaranteed for the following several years. This allows the operators to set high-confidence expectations of revenues, and to benefit from accurate future financial planning.

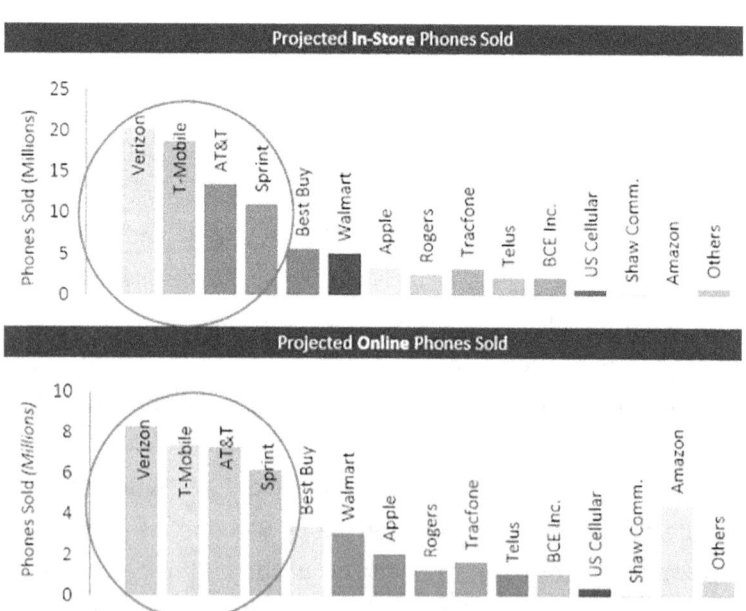

Back to the challenge in Asia. It turns out that payment method there for the monthly use of the cellular network is in most cases is prepaid. What are the implications of this?

Unlike most European countries or North America, the vast majority of Asian mobile users pay in advance rather than at the end of each month; use of the network is prepaid and not postpaid, and this has implications for our products. In most cases, the user purchases the phone from retail chains, so that the cellular operator does not really have an incentive to sell phones, because it would do so only if that tied the user to the operator, by way of their commitment to use its mobile network. If a customer pays in advance for a package of calls and surfing the web, then, towards the end of using the package, they can reconsider which operator they will buy the next package from. In other words – it is very difficult for the cellular operator to create customer commitment when payment is prepaid. Also, as far as the customer is concerned, they have no reason to purchase the phone in the cellular operator's stores, so they would consider buying their next phone in retail stores instead.

The business model for retailers who are not cellular operators is completely different. While the cellular operators are interested in the monthly payment for using the cellular network, and selling the phone is another tool to achieve this, for other retailers, the emphasis is to profit from the sale itself, so there is very high sensitivity to the cost of the sale, which reduces our chances to sell them hardware-based products that are relatively expensive. What more, the retailers want to charge the consumer for providing them with our capabilities. That is, it seems that the retailers are willing to pay us, but only on the basis of payment per transaction: if the customer wants to use our service, they pay the retailer $5, for example, and the retailer will pay us a smaller nominal amount for the transaction. Such a model does not require an initial investment on the retailer's part, and nevertheless allows it to provide quality service, which it also profits from.

But bottom line, because we sell both software and hardware, and we have a big investment (the hardware) that we must make sure we cover within a certain period of time, we cannot charge only for the transaction, since no one is willing to guaranty us that in a given time period, enough transactions will be made to return our investment for the hardware. Therefore, **our current product is not suitable for the Asian market.**

This is an example of a situation in which management must make a decision whether to close its activity in a given market, due to the discovery of a discrepancy between the product and the existing business model in that market, or alternatively, to maintain a low level activity, assuming that in the work plan for the near future, a suitable product could be developed. I was not ready to make this decision at this stage.

Japan

I got to know Japan in the previous spin-off I managed; then, I established my business activity with the help of a local sales representative. During that period, I participated in many meetings, mainly for the purpose of selecting distribution partners, and with potential customers who were mobile operators. The result was only limited sales.

Current sales in Japan were mainly to second and third tier companies, which were the retail arm of small local cellular companies or of large retail networks. Annual sales were only on the level of several hundred thousand dollars, with marginal profitability.

A number of interesting points about Japan and the work there:

- In terms of consumer payments, this is a postpaid market, as in most of the US and Western Europe.
- Japan is a country with a very strong retail orientation. It has nearly 20,000 stores which sell cellphones, of which close to 5,000 sell "second hand" phones.
- The sales process profile is long. Foreign companies will find it difficult to sell without local representation and the simple reason – Japanese customers usually rely more on local companies, so that for the most part they will insist that a local company is the one that makes the sale and is responsible for providing service.
- Customers are very strict about quality and consistency in performance.
- I will not elaborate here on the unique behavior procedures in business meetings or, in general on the subject of manners in Japan, but I have a warm recommendation – do not start business activity in Japan without an escort to guide you in terms of accepted behavior, at least in the first meetings.

The company that represented us in Japan served at that time as an exclusive distributor.

Unlike Singapore, I designated Japan as an important potential target for our current products for several reasons:

1. **Gadgets market** – The Japanese are very fond of purchasing the next thing, especially when it comes to electronics, and that includes cellphones.

   The higher the frequency of phone purchases, the greater the need for our products, and we must remember that Japan has a population of more than 120 million people.

2. **Population age** – On the other hand, Japan has a very large elderly population, and as we get older, the tendency to

consume changes decreases, so the number of old type cellphones (feature phones) among this population is very large. One of the essential advantages of our current hardware platform is its ability to read data from feature phones.

3. **Sensitivity to information security** – expressed on two levels:

- In Japan, there is a serious concern of using an external cloud to store user's cellphone information. It is very hard to convince operators about this, as of the beginning of 2018.

   Here, we had an advantage – on our dedicated hardware platform, it was possible to transfer information between cellphones without a network connection, and thus to ensure the non-leakage of information.

- Japan has a well-developed industry selling second-hand cellphones, but they require a "deep" erasure of old information. It is important to understand that there are a number of levels of deleting information on cellphones. Information recoverability is of course very much related to the operating system and how old the phone is, but at the present, you can recover information from most cellphones, even from those which were ostensibly erased (this is less true for IOS systems).

   We had a technology that made it possible to irreversibly erase information from a cellphone, which also worked for Android systems, which should be very interesting to this big market in Japan.

At a meeting in Japan, I was able to meet with the person in the distribution company who was responsible for selling our products, and their staff. I also had a meeting with a number of customers.

During the internal meeting, several requests, and several worrisome diagnoses, were raised:

1. **The structure of the company that represents us** is a structure that is still prevalent in Japanese companies, but is fundamentally different from the structure of Western companies active in Japan. Two examples in regard to Japanese companies that complement each other: (a) From the moment they hire you, they will not fire you, unless you decide to leave. (b) On the other hand, salaries are significantly lower than those paid to employees in parallel positions in Western companies active in Japan. In addition to low wages, there is no adequate compensation for working difficult hours, such as if you worked 14 hours one day, or on a weekend, something which happens quite a bit. In addition, and this is most worrying: there is no real compensation for making a sale, so there's really nothing to motivate employees, especially salespeople, to go above and beyond the call of duty.

   In general, a model according to which the employee's salary is not affected by the fact that they worked 8 hours per day or 14 hours, and if they achieved lukewarm results or amazing results – they would earn the same amount – would, in my opinion, bring mediocre employees to such a place of work, especially currently, when many Western companies are active in Japan, and employees hear from their colleagues about the different conditions in Western companies.

2. **Harsh complaints about our high prices in Japan.** When I asked to understand in depth how they came to the conclusion that our prices are high, they spread before me two local competitors whose prices, on the face of it, are 30% lower than ours. I decided to stop everything and invest the following hours analyzing with them, in depth, what the competitors really offer and what their business model was. After a few hours, there was a clear understanding that our competitors

offered only a partial solution, and one not suitable for the new phones that have come out on the market in the past two years. What was more severe in terms of their lack of depth in analyzing the data – our competitors also charged extra for every new phone released to the local market, which in terms of price made theirs identical to ours.

As a result of our visit, we decided, several weeks later, on the following moves regarding the Japanese market:

- To recruit someone to be our representative in Japan who would be compensated by Western standards, and would manage the distributor while themselves participating in meetings with potential customers.

- To make changes to the original distribution agreement in keeping with Western standards, including cancellation of the exclusivity, as well as reducing the commission to the distributor by 50%, which should contribute significantly to improving our profitability.

- Despite the harsh complaints about our high prices, and after the discussion I detailed, I decided to raise prices by 20%. According to all the indications I had, the local market would absorb this increase.

- To double the sales target for 2017 to one million dollars, and set it at three million dollars for 2018. The backlog of opportunities supported these values.

The United States

I knew the US well; I had established a business activity there in the past. In practice, the main business activity of all the companies I managed, or in which I served a key position, was in the US, so it's a place where I feel at home.

The meeting with employees in the US was especially important, because the US market accounted for 55% of MLC's revenues, and yet I expected that the atmosphere in meetings with the employees would be tense, with claims and comments similar to those I had heard many times over the last month. So at this point, when the challenges the company faced were already clearly focused, I decided to show them the challenges before I let them express themselves. It was important for me to show our employees that I thoroughly understand the condition of the company, and to display a framework of my timetable for providing a plan to deal with the challenges that were clear to all.

Steve Altman, who led the business in North America, had joined the company almost two years before, and managed a team of 11 people, most of whom were salespeople, and he was a full partner in planning the meeting.

By raising the challenges and difficulties we must solve, and by the very fact that I proved that I understood them, we succeeded in creating hope. Of course, even after that, the employees repeatedly emphasized the problems, but the complaint session was like just an additional show.

The uneasy feelings of the employees concerned mainly the following areas:

1. Our company does not innovate – the technological lead the company had enjoyed for years had eroded. The company only responds to individual cases for market needs.

2. Our company's vision is unclear – we do not know what will happen in another year or two.

3. Unready products are released – it appears that a new product that came out to support companies that repair cellphones in large volumes was completely unprepared.

4. A disconnection exists between the field and the product managers – that is, market demands that arrive from the US do not receive a response.

At the end of the visit, I committed myself to return to meet with them within three months, in order to present a clear plan that would address the issues raised.

Brazil

Our Brazilian office has been active for a number of years, and supports our operations throughout South America.

Business activity in South America has its own pace, which is in most cases slow compared to Europe or North America.

In the past, in the framework of one of my previous companies, I considered investing in order to penetrate South America with a center in Brazil, but I decided against this move because of the cost of import taxes and the complex and complicated bureaucracy involved in imports, and also because of how complicated everything connected to the employment of local employees was in Brazil.

In general, before the trip, I checked once again a number of parameters that bothered me regarding this market:

1. **Import tariffs** – In Brazil, which accounts for 50% of the continent's population, customs duties on imports of hardware as of 2016 were between 50% and 100%, which doubles the cost of our products compared to North America or Europe.

2. **Accounting bureaucracy** – accounting and bureaucratic complexity in Brazil, according to available business management studies, it is 11 times that of Western countries, a fact that requires huge attention.

3. **Prepayments** – As on the trip to Singapore, I checked in advance the percentage of prepayments, and found that here, too, in South America, the vast majority of mobile users pay in advance, rather than at the end of each month.

A major reason for prepayment in South America is the big difference in the price of a call there if it is made between two different cellular operators or the same operator. The problematic aspect there, as far as we are concerned, is the same as in Asia, where in most cases the user purchases the phone from retail networks and the cellular operator has no incentive to sell phones, because it cannot tie the user to the operator. As mentioned above, retailers must profit from the sale itself, and therefore there is a very high sensitivity to the cost of the sale, which reduces our chances to sell hardware-based products at a price that will allow us to earn a profit, because the cost of these products is relatively high. What's more, for the capabilities that we provide, there is a desire to charge the consumer for those services. It appears that retailers would be willing to pay us for this, but only per transaction, i.e., after the provision of the service, and not before, which would allow the retailer to provide quality service that it also profits from, similar to the situation in Asia. At the present time, we did not have an option to support sales per transaction, and we will expand on that later.

In terms of the general indications I cited, the chances of success, given the company's current products and operating costs, were not high.

What complicated the situation in South America was the fact that the company won a tender offered by one of the largest cellular companies on the continent, and with a number of difficult restrictions:

- Brazil, the largest country in South America, with 220 million residents, was not included in the agreement.
- Apart from an indication of quantities, which are only the potential of the purchase by that operator, there was no actual commitment to purchase our products.
- In addition to the general agreement, the company was required to sign an additional agreement with each country separately.
- There was a commitment under the contract, for support, and making product improvements in several dimensions.

I would not recommend signing a contract that defines requirements for performance from the supplier, but without the purchaser having an obligation to purchase defined amounts of the supplier's products.

Total sales in South America were low, and although the target for bookings for 2016 amounted to a significant number of millions of dollars, in practice, after seven months into the year, sales were below 20% of our target.

This is not a simple situation.

Summary of the visits to offices abroad

Beyond getting to know of the managers and employees abroad personally, understanding our situation vis-à-vis competitors and business models contributed greatly to the consolidation of a strategic plan over the coming months. The essential points which I noted for myself as a result of the packed series of visits were as follows:

1. We provide a market solution (sales in stores) that will continue to decline, since more buyers are turning to online channels.

We will need a different kind of solution to increase our target markets.

2. In most cases where the model for the sale of cellular packages is paid in advance, our current solution is not suitable, since we do not support payment per transaction. Thus, we invest a lot of effort and money in markets that will not yield a profit, until we adapt our products and their pricing model as is necessary.

3. There is a disconnect from the market; information from the field does not arrive, and our understanding of the dynamics of the market is deficient.

4. It is not clear to the employees where the company is going, and how it will regain product-technological leadership.

Building the lead team

Managers usually look for positive figures, those who move things forward – ones who, on the one hand, are not deterred by any challenge, but on the other hand, who move at the ground level. Ones who are not blind to difficulties, who do not jump from cliffs with no deep water below them, but ones who are looking for a challenge, a problem whose solution will lead to a breakthrough, who seek to solve difficult riddles without fear of failure.

It is always interesting to be present in the dynamics of a discussion about a problem that is a difficulty but also an opportunity, and see on the one hand the "optimistic attackers," and on the other hand, the "pessimistic defenders." On the one hand, there are those who are looking for any way to solve problems and are not afraid to go out on a limb, in accordance with their ideas, and on the other hand, there are those who consistently explain why every idea proposed will not succeed, or greatly stress the risks involved. The ideal combination, the optimal composition, includes a mixture of both types in the dosage which represents the spirit of the leader.

In choosing a lead team, each CEO has their own credo as to what is required of each of the leaders in order that as a team, the members will complement and strengthen each other, and will lead to an optimal result. Critical and cautious voices must be heard within the team, but the team must be built in such a way that those voices do not diminish or dampen the team spirit, but rather contribute to its success.

Personally, I have five parameters that are mandatory for a lead team member. Each manager will set their own weight of each of the following factors, but to me, a leader must be excellent in each and every one of them.

Leadership

1. A manager with a leadership capacity is someone capable of moving things forward, especially things that are difficult and complex.

   What is included in the concept of "leading things forward?"

   ♦ Understanding the need to explain (market) and convince (sell) the process.

   ♦ Precise planning, with all its intra- and extra-organizational implications.

   ♦ Execution.

2. A leader will increase motivation among their subordinates and will inspire them to follow them willingly, because they believe that the manager will lead them to new heights, and not only out of necessity, stemming from the manager's seniority or authority.

3. A leader is someone who will bring their subordinates to adopt the target of the project and its goals, so that they will feel a personal commitment no less than the leader's.

4. Leadership, in my view, includes initiative and resourcefulness, being the first to recognize a potential problem, finding the cure before the disease strikes.

5. A leader's need to delegate authority is considered trivial and obvious, but in practice, delegation of authority is not sufficiently widespread. A good leader knows how to delegate authority with the aim of giving their subordinates a sense that they are partners in the group's success. Delegation of authority creates a sense of responsibility in the employees, increases their motivation to advance the group and the entire company, and creates group pride. In addition, delegating authority allows avoidance of bottlenecks in decision-making, which delays the progress of the group and therefore the whole company.

Teamwork

1. A good manager knows how to productively resolve conflicts with other managers.

2. A good manager is businesslike and practical in discussions with other managers on their level; they do not insist on a certain position only because of the difficulty in accepting other opinions.

Professionalism

Professionalism is a very broad word that can be defined in many ways and in different dimensions.

The ten most important aspects of a professional manager include:

1. Respecting the company you work for and the managers who work with you.

2. Being organized and purposeful.

3. Clear communication between the manager and the team.

4. Avoiding organizational politics.
5. Having a thorough and comprehensive knowledge and understanding of their work.
6. Establishing a clear vision regarding the direction in which they lead their group, and what is the "next thing" to be pursued in the realm of the group's activity.
7. Ability to quickly diagnose and learn changes and trends in the area of their group activity.
8. Striving to be at the forefront of innovation.
9. Ability to solve problems that arise during work, and knowing how to overcome obstacles in a way that advances the company.
10. Studying subjects that are beyond their responsibility, so that they can contribute to important organizational decisions.

"The optimistic attackers"

A good manager should be positive about the challenges, including the most difficult and the most problematic ones.

A manager needs to manage challenges in a balanced way; they must thoroughly and in-depth examine all the relevant information, but most of the energy must be directed toward finding solutions, rather than toward expressing concern of what will be the result in case of failure.

The commitment to win

A manager should be committed to winning – to achieving the goal.

There are times when you need the "extra effort," even if it causes "pain," and managers who are committed to achieving the goal do not think twice, but are simply focused on doing everything needed in order to achieve their goal. Whether it's the sales manager who, after a series of meetings with a customer abroad, comes to the conclusion that he should stay with the customer for further meetings to ensure winning the project, which hinders their return home and challenges them in their personal life; or the development team's realization that in order to release a new product to the market, they will have to work around the clock for a few days, and it's clear to the manager that there is no other way.

Ross Pero once said: "When I build a team, first I look for people who love to win. If there are none, I look for people who hate to lose."

The executive team

The lead team – the executive team, are the ones who determine the goals of the organization, and are responsible for achieving those goals. They have the tools, and they have the responsibility, which they can take upon themselves or delegate to others; therefore, they are the most important people in the organization.

I mentioned above the basic qualities required of managers, which for me are necessary during recruitment of the executive team.

In addition, it's important for me to make sure that none of the leading individuals have emotional ties to what has been developed so far, especially if he or she thinks that the current product is of high quality, while you as a manager think differently.

It is difficult to exaggerate the readiness of people to defend decisions, products, or ideas they have given of their time and energy to. We tend to develop a layer of feelings toward decisions we have made, certainly toward those in which we invested strenuous work, whether by persuading others or by the many hours we spent on them, and by the private time that we have sacrificed for them. Out of all this, a deep emotional bond is formed with everything that we have created through thought and action, but in many cases – all this is not really tied to the quality of the end result.

It was important to me that the difficult decisions before us be quickly accepted, and from an objective perspective not influenced by any emotion or irrelevant motives.

I sought, among other things, where possible and subject to the quality of the candidate, to take advantage of the opportunity to add new members to the executive team who had not yet served as vice presidents, and more importantly – had not yet sat around the executive table. The goal was twofold: to create motivation among those who join, and help those with the right skills to take another step in building their career.

There are many models for managing a company, and we will not deal here with this broad and important issue, but I will note that I believe and advocate a very active involvement of all members of the executive team. I aim to hear a wide range of opinions before making a decision, and accordingly, I expect the members of the executive team to express their views clearly, and defend what they believe in professionally and fearlessly. But – and this is an indisputable "but" – from the moment a decision is made, each member of management must accept it and even present it and defend it in any discussion, even if originally they opposed it.

Presenting a united front vis-ā-vis employee, customers, the board of directors, or anybody in general, is not subject to compromise, for only thus is it possible to carry out processes that require great resources and force, in order to achieve far-reaching goals for the organization. That is, discussions and arguments during management meetings are necessary to make good decisions, but once the decision is made, everyone must get in line and demonstrate a united front.

I too, personally, had the opportunity to make quite a few decisions that were contrary to my original opinion, as a result of pointed, businesslike discussions.

In addition, it is important to remember that a company is not a democratic body. There is one head; in the end, I have to make decisions whose results are reviewed by the board of directors. However, the CEO's results are largely determined by the quality of the executive team, and its contribution to the management of the company.

The CEO is a kind of orchestral conductor; they can control the tempo, the harmony of sounds, but they must have high-quality musicians on their side, to bring to an optimum the emphases they want to get across.

In what order is the lead team constructed?

In an organization that expects to reach annual sales of many tens of millions of dollars in the near future, all executive functions must be fully covered.

My credo is that to succeed, and to achieve global leadership, in general, we must produce technological leadership. (It is important to note that there are quite a few exceptions, technology companies that succeeded even without technological leadership; each case must be examined on its own merits).

What is success? Every organization has its definition of success, but in my view, as a goal, succeeding is being the number one in income and profits in your field. In an organization of our size, 150 people who live in a high cost of living area, it is difficult to achieve success without clear technological leadership and without a vision which will support progress and growth for at least the next three years.

With such a credo, the first decision was to choose the R&D leader.

Head of Research and Development

As part of the initial round of interviews, I met with the former R&D executive vice president of the two divisions, and the R&D VP under him, who was in charge of the MLC, both very high-quality people. In practice, several meetings were held, some of which focused mainly on product demonstration. During the meetings, we discussed, and questioned, the quality of the code and the awkwardness of the user experience.

In the context of the pressures stemming from the need to develop capabilities that were requested by, and promised to our customers, it was clear that a lack of development time, which was repeated in every version, was certainly the basis for the constraints that drove the company to maintain an overly complex software platform. However, the managers' defensiveness in regard to this situation, and the lack of recognition of a red line beyond which the code must be rewritten, or at least fighting to dedicate designated resources to it, bothered me greatly.

After much thought, I decided to recruit a new vice president for R&D who was not bound emotionally to everything that had been developed so far.

It is important to emphasize that "speed to market" is always critical, especially if the product has something that is not only unique but innovative, while it is also known that the market is demanding, and waiting for, a solution, waiting for that first company which will make the innovative solution accessible to the market.

That is, the level of innovation or uniqueness of a new product that is intended for launching will be harmed if the product does not reach the market before competitors. Slow speed to market is comparable to conceding the competitive advantage to the company's competitors. Innovation and speed to market go hand in hand; one without the other is of little value.

Here there is always a dilemma – whether to invest in thorough development or to produce something quickly on a temporary infrastructure, in order to be the first in the market. Perhaps it's better to risk delaying the initial arrival to the market, but to reach it with a strong infrastructure, one that will allow future flexibility, enabling the development team to make changes and expand faster in the future. I call this dilemma the "infrastructure dilemma."

In many cases where the original (and correct) decision of launching a new and unique capability based on a temporary infrastructure, in order to speed up the release to the market was made – subsequently, the time and resources needed to develop the same capability on an in-depth and high-quality infrastructure were not given, although they should have been. Over time, this is one of the main causes of a cumbersome software infrastructure.

After interviews with five candidates, Moshe Lipsker, who for the past 15 years had been a senior R&D manager in an American technology company, where he led more than 100 developers from a number of disciplines, was chosen to be the new R&D VP.

Indeed, working 15 years in one place can attest to a disadvantage, but as one who worked nearly 14 years in the same place, I can testify that in a dynamic environment which is continuously changing, working for a long time in the same place is almost irrelevant.

The challenge of leadership in R&D was our most essential challenge. In the difficult and fragile process that had to be moved forward in a group of market-desirable R&D employees who had worked for many years under the same managers, managers who would soon be replaced. Therefore, Moshe Lipsker's experience in the complex management of engineers from different countries, with the complexity of different behaviors in different countries, along with his strong experience in command of an elite unit in the army, helped me a lot in my decision to select him.

Quality Assurance Manager

The next job to be filled was the VP of quality assurance, a non-trivial choice, mainly because the thought was to shift to Agile methodology.

One may ask: Since this development methodology integrates the QA group into the development process, why was there a need to have a separate leader for the QA team?

The answer is that it was important to me to maintain a QA group that is independent of R&D, and capable of stopping the release of a defective product or version, in accordance with established quality standards.

This group had three main functions:

1. **QA**

QA, Quality Assurance, Quality Control – this is a concept that every organization will define in accordance with its requirements.

The narrowest view relates to the quality control of the company's product.

The QA personnel are responsible for carrying out the software tests, from the beginning of the product development process to the final stage. The QA personnel are responsible to ensure that the product will reach the customer without flaws and without malfunctions, while preserving the rules and processes defined by the organization.

From a broader perspective, this responsibility will also include organizational processes. Here are a number of important processes as an example:

- Software release process.
- Product definition process.
- Product launch process.
- How to address customer complaints and many other important organizational processes.

2. **Customer Support**

Customer support includes a range of customer services whose purpose is to help in the operation of the product in regard to installation, training, assistance in malfunctions, and more. There are different levels of customer support; what differentiates between them is usually connected to support hours, work days, response times and the variety of languages. We will elaborate on this later.

3. **Customer Success**

Customer Success - In one of the first reports I asked for, I saw that our software license renewal rates are very low, around 50%. There was no clear answer given to the question as to why this was; instead, a long list of reasons was given, without any objective factual basis.

The purpose of the Customer Success function is to closely monitor the level and quality of use of the product (which functionality is used more, and which less), so that, according to the results of the monitoring, we can discover defects in usability, or problems in the product. The information is passed to the product management group with recommendations for one change or another, to the QA team if a bug is discovered, or to customer support so that they can explain to the customer how using the product differently will bring them better results.

In addition, it is the responsibility of this function to communicate regularly with representative customers, to learn from them about their user-experience with the product.

The Customer Success group's performance is measured by the level of customer use, which in most cases will be translated directly to the license renewal rate.

Of the many candidates for the position, I chose Yoni Danieli. Yoni had rich experience in leading a QA team in a variety of companies, including leadership in a company that develops secure cellphones. I identified in him all the five elements a leader needs, as I mentioned above; furthermore, what he was looking for in a job was to be influential, and membership in our executive management team would certainly allow him to have an impact.

Product management leader

In the section "Meetings with employees", the role of the product manager was described in detail. As mentioned, this area is the most important and complex one in the organization, since the product manager should also set the organization's direction in everything related to markets, products, and business models, and they actively reach into each of the organization's other departments.

The impact of the Product VP on the success of the organization is most significant. The critical decisions are made by the company's entire senior management, but the Product VP should be the main source that brings information about, and requests regarding the product to the senior management for decision.

Imagine that the company decides to develop a product based on a certain technology which at the end of the process the market does not adopt. This can result in the end of the company, or at least its suffering a blow that will take it a long time to recover from.

There are endless examples of this, and here are some prominent ones: videotapes in the 1990s: VCR versus 8 mm, or some film camera manufacturers' delay in entering the field of digital cameras, and there are many other cases.

In small and medium-sized companies, the influence of the decision to develop a product is critical. What product manager has not encountered the situation in which they are facing an important customer who is sharing with them the new directions they are considering, and who recommends that they adjust their products accordingly? The product manager who accepts the request – if a decision had been already made whereby the company is improving or expanding its product line in the same direction as the customer indicated, then they are in good shape, since they just received a tailwind and approval from an important customer regarding that decision. But what happens if the product manager doesn't think the customer's recommendation is in the right direction? Refusing the customer's suggestion may mean losing a central and important customer, which is expressed not only in a significant loss of income, but also in a loss of a reference by which they can persuade new customers. On the other hand, acceding to the customer's demand means committing development, and the whole organization, to launching a product that the company does not believe will help it to move toward the goal it has set for itself. That is, if it develops the requested product, the company will probably keep the important customer, but it may, because of this, arrive late to the market with the products and developments which are important to it, and thus harm its strategic plans. This is a dilemma which we face regularly. The product manager is the one that must bring all the data and their recommendation to the company management, and hence the product manager's great importance.

In the current organizational situation, it was clear to me that I intended to be involved in the details of any decision of this group and reshape it over time, so I decided at this point to leave the product management group as it was and promote Amir Shani, who was one of the product managers, to the position of Product Management VP.

Sales

I had interviewed most of the sales people, with an emphasis on the US and Europe. My impression was that they were professionals, and therefore I decided to promote people from within the company.

I have lived in the US for many years and set up sales entities there which were a combination of direct sales and distribution channels. I also lived a parallel period in Europe and Asia for the same purpose, and I found differences in many parameters between the two regions.

It is important to note some notable differences between sales management in Europe and the United States:

1. Language – Although it depends on the area of business, basically the United States is one big country with one language, in contrast to Europe, where, in most cases, speakers of an additional language will be required if your goal is to sell in France, England, Germany, Spain or Italy.

2. Recruitment of local salespeople – The employment terms structure is almost identical throughout the United States,

but this is not the case in Europe. Not only will the salaries in different countries be different, but fringe benefits, employment laws, and termination procedures also differ significantly from country to country.

3. Working from home – In the US, working from home is very common among salespeople. In Europe this is not always so, in many countries, especially in the urban regions, people prefer to work from offices. There are a number reasons for this, the simplest most obvious among them being that in the US homes are larger than in Europe, making it easier to work from home.

Given the size of the company, I decided to divide the world into two:

- America (North and South).
- Asia + EMEA (Europe, Middle East, and Africa).

Each area would be managed by a single sales leader, with the two leaders being members of senior management and reporting to me. However, not all changes would begin immediately.

America

Our current business activity in North America was managed by Steve Altman, as part of a team of 11 people. Since the US contributed 55% of the company's revenues, while the contribution of South America was minimal, in order not to divert focus from the North America manager, I decided to initially manage sales in South America myself. This move should also enable me to explore the real potential of this market, with the understanding that until we come up with new platforms which fit the business model in South America, revenues will be low. In practice, this region indeed contributed very little to the total annual revenue of the company.

I had great doubts about our ability to succeed in South America. As I explained in a previous chapter, in South America, most cellphone users pay in advance for using the phone, (prepaid) and not at the end of each month. What's more, for the capabilities we provide, the retailers want to charge the consumer for providing our service. The indications were that retailers would be willing to pay us part of this charge, but only according to a model of payment per transaction, i.e., after the provision of the service, and not before it, which will enable the retailer to provide quality service that it also profits from. At this stage we did not have an option to support sales per transaction; the lack of this option was expected to limit sales in the region.

I gave myself six months to figure out what to do in South America, if anything at all: what the right business model is, what the organizational structure should be, and which products we could market there. Only after clarification of these fundamental issues would it be possible to connect it to North America.

Europe and Asia

Until I joined the company, the European operations of the MLC division were artificially divided into the DACH countries (Germany, Austria, and Switzerland) and the rest of Europe. The reason for this was historical and irrelevant to us at this stage, so I decided to unite all of Europe under one manager, Alon Schnitzer, who for the previous three years ran all of Europe except for the DACH countries.

In addition, I also assigned all of Asia, apart from Japan, to Alon, with the understanding that, as in South America, we would initially put Asia on a low profile, until we formulated a detailed plan for this region. The exception to this policy in Asia was Japan, where I have a lot of experience, so in this case as well, I took the management of Japan upon myself.

The bottom line was that in the two main markets we had two spearheads, not one.

Marketing

I was impressed by Jade Kahn's professional work and previous experience as an analyst, and despite his youth, I decided to give him the opportunity to take the reins and build up the marketing activity from scratch, on a new foundation, and with a new orientation.

It is important to emphasize that at this stage, since no target plan had yet been formulated for business activity beyond financial targets for the current budget year, it was not possible to define which changes were required within the focus of the marketing activity.

Finance

Ido Tzur served as VP finance for both divisions of the original company; he reported to the CFO and everyone agreed that he would come to work for us and set up the finance department of the MLC company. This was a very important acquisition that allowed us a smooth transition to establish our finance department.

VP Finance is considered one of the key positions in any organization. This position is in charge of managing the important resource – money, with all that this implies: auditing income and expenses, cash flow, budgetary control, control of taxes, auditing the work of the organization's accountants and bookkeepers, and, of course, making preparations for external audits. All these are only a sample of the overall role of the head of finance.

In addition, every issue of raising capital and regular updates to the Board of Directors will be based on his work.

As in most hi-tech companies, we also intended that the finance VP would be responsible for both agreements and business contracts. This also provided a good opportunity for Ido to deal with subjects he wanted to accumulate rich experience in, mainly in legal matters, very complex contracts, and there was also initial thinking to subordinate the IT area to him.

Human Resources

The definition of the profession – human resources – assumes that the company's employees are a resource, just like the rest of the organization's resources, and therefore must be managed efficiently, economically, and professionally. The role of human resources manager is a strategic one, and some will say that they are one of the most important and most essential professionals in the organization. This is the job that is responsible in a variety of ways to manage, recruit, develop and conserve the organization's human capital. Conserving human capital sounds trivial, but its impact on the organization's ability to meet its objectives is great. Because of the importance of this subject, I will deal with it in some detail:

In high-tech companies, human resources are the most important and expensive resources. When we look at the expenses of the organization in a given budget year, we will discover that in most (software) companies, the financial expenditure on human resources is 70-90% of total expenditure.

If we take a company with 50 employees, 15 of whom leave it within one year, the implications of this will be expressed on several levels, such as, for example, a significant departure of knowledge from the organization. In a technological organization, most of the knowledge is possessed by the employees, and when they leave, the knowledge leaves with them. When we recruit a replacement for an employee who left, it will be months before the replacement acquires the level of knowledge that the employee they replaced had, no matter in what field: company products, development methods, sales, competitors... in fact, in any field. It happens quite often that one employee, or a limited number of employees, possess very unique knowledge, so that when they leave, the damage can be very heavy.

That's why the subject of human resource retention is so important. How is it possible to reach a high employee retention level? Much deep thought must be devoted to this subject, which takes into consideration many parameters that here is not the place to expand upon, but I will mention a few important things:

- In the recruitment process, you must understand what motivates the candidate to search for a new job: wages and conditions, promotion, study and personal development, influence, job security, company environment or any other reason. Every organization has its strengths: a healthy social environment, advanced technology and more. A match (and preferably a very strong match) must exist between the candidate's motive and the strengths of the organization.

- The match must also be examined at the level of the applicant's ability to cope over time with the type of challenges and nature of the work environment – in our case, for example, there are many customers at any given time who are not satisfied.

  When customers complain regularly, this creates mental stress in employees working with an ongoing interface with those customers. The ability of the candidate to meet the pressures, if they are included in the interface group, is very important both for them and for the employees in their vicinity.

- Beyond the impact of the loss of knowledge, large-scale departure produces an atmosphere of disintegration. The employees ask themselves: If so many are leaving, why am I staying? Is there anything happening here that I, as an employee in one of the departments, do not understand? Why doesn't the company respond to the situation that has come about? What does this mean? That is, a snowball effect begins to form, a snowball that is gaining momentum, and as time passes, more energy will be required to stop it, so it's better to stop it as soon as possible.

As I mentioned, there are other important parameters in evaluating the employee-job match that we will not elaborate on. One important thing to do is – set up a realistic target for employee retention. That is, in the real world, even though a company's senior management company will take actions to improve employee retention, nevertheless, employees will leave. What the company does need to do is to set a numerical goal for departures per year, and at the end of each year to examine the number of employee departures in reality and the reasons for them, so that we can improve.

I recommend taking one more step in defining the employee retention target: mapping and defining who are the key employees in the organization. There are employees in an organization whose departure will cause more significant damage, compared to others. The recommendation is to identify who they are, and set a more challenging retention target for them as compared to other employees. Each organization will define to himself who the key employees are, but as a rule of thumb, they will be approximately 10% of all employees.

We received support in regards to everything related to human resources from the company headquarters, which supported us admirably. They provided all the help we needed, whether in the framework of recruiting new managers or in parting with some of the managers.

As the weeks passed and the process of change began, I felt the lack of a human resources manager function that would report to me and will be dedicated to the newly created company. There were quite a few changes that I intended to make, both personnel changes and organizational changes, in the HQ and abroad. Similarly, I wanted to ensure that there was someone who would lead the whole issue of employee retention at a time when so many changes were taking place. In general, I felt the need for ongoing HR assistance with my work and working with division managers.

We added Lily Rom at the end of the year as Human Resources Manager. Here too, we recruited a woman with promising abilities, who until now had worked in large companies attached to one of the departments or divisions, and in our new company was given the opportunity to lead this important role on the entire organizational level.

To sum up the issue of building the lead team: we had eight leaders, VP's, all of whom were new around the management table: three new recruits (R&D, Quality, Human Resources), four who were promoted through their activities in the MLC division (Marketing, EMEA + Asia Sales, USA sales, Product Management) and one who worked previously in the overall company's headquarters (Finance).

Business strategy – image and reality

One of the important things to do when you enter a senior management position is to check whether there is a close match between the stated business strategy of the company and the actual situation.

A company's business strategy defines what the company is planning to do in order to meet its business objectives for a period of several years.

Business strategy affects every employee in every department, every work plan, and every intermediate goal that the company sets for itself. It touches every significant area, such as organizational and managerial structure, management processes, process control, business orientation, and more. Setting up a business strategy is a basic and essential activity, but it's equally essential to check if the business strategy is actually executed.

Over the years, I have seen many promising companies fail because of a lack of compatibility between what they defined for themselves as organizational culture and business strategy, and what the company's actual conduct. It turns out that it's often very easy to think that a company is one thing, when in reality it is something else, and the gap between image and reality may serve as a fertile breeding ground for a variety of problems and a lack of clarity.

The following pages will examine different aspects of business strategy and the meaning of each of them, and then we will discuss the condition of the company I was managing, comparing the goals it had defined for itself with what was actually happening, in regards to the following aspects of strategy:

1. Profitability or growth.
2. Off-the-shelf or customized product.
3. One territory or global activity.
4. Patent registration - yes or no.

It is important to note that there are many other aspects and areas included in the framework of company business strategy, but this book will limit itself to the four listed topics.

Profitability or growth

A company can define as its business strategy the aspiration to be profitable at any given moment – in contrast to a strategy that emphasizes business growth, for example. If a company defines its main objective as presenting an increase in business each month or in any quarter/year, this will have a completely different effect on its conduct than if it had defined as a strategic goal to focus on profitability, rather than business growth.

The two approaches – profitability and growth – find it difficult to coexist, and many times a contradiction will arise between them. However, in order to understand the challenge, we must define what is growth; there are quite a few indices for this.

Business increase can be measured periodically (for example, once a month and/or quarterly and/or annually) by one or a combination of some of the following ways, for example:

- Number of active customers.
- New customers added.
- Number of new orders.
- Total revenue.
- Total sales (booking).
- Average sales growth per customer (upsell).
- MRR - Monthly Recurring Revenue.
  This refers to a monthly turnover of the company from customers who have subscriptions, mainly in reference to software products in a SaaS (Software as a Service) licensing model.
- ARR - Annual Recurring Revenue, similar to MRR but the annual turnover of the company from customers who have subscriptions.

- Annual Contract Value (ACV) is the average price of an annual contract to the customer. This calculation does not include one-time payments.

    For example, if a customer signed a three-year contract for $36,000, the ACV of that customer is $12,000.

    If the company has 100 customers who produce monthly income from subscription fees of $1,000 per month, the ACV is also $12,000.

    The ACV is not very revealing in itself, but it becomes especially important when it's compared to other values. If you compare the ACV to the average annual cost to 'purchase' a customer (cost of acquisition), you will see how long it takes to return the cost of acquiring a customer.

Here is another example, and this time we'll compare ACV to ARR.

Customer A

The customer purchased an annual license at $1,000 per year.

Values calculated for customer A only:

ARR = $1,000

ACV = $1,000

Customer B

The customer purchased an annual license at $750 per year.

Values calculated for customer B only:

ARR = $750

ACV = $750

Customer C

The customer purchased an annual license at a price of $500 per year.

Values calculated for customer C only:

ARR = $500

ACV = $500

Calculating indices for all three customers:

ARR: $1,000 + $750 + $500 = $2,250

ACV: ($1,000 + $750 + $500) / 3 = $750

There are, of course, many other indicators that we will not mention.

Returning to business growth, let's consider the following example:

We have a product that we sell to 200 large companies. These companies are very satisfied, and some of them ask us to develop a complementary product which will suit most of our customers. On the face of it, this is good news; responding to such a request would increase the company's future revenue level, would increase the revenue from the customer, and may even position us as a one-stop shop, all this along with other potential advantages. But on the other hand, it demands investments: increasing the development team, increasing the product management team and the support system, and more. In other words, it is a decision that requires an immediate increase in expenses, whose revenues will arrive only after many months, and in some cases after years. In many cases, taking such a step is likely to cause the company to suffer a deep short-term loss. If the strategy of the company is to be profitable at any given moment, the expansion process described here would potentially cause it to have a year of financial loss. Therefore, if the company acts in accordance with its profit-based business strategy, it is reasonable to assume that it will hold off on the suggested development until it accumulates sufficient money to make the necessary investment.

It is important to understand that there is no statement here as to which strategy is more correct, that's an absolutely irrelevant question. My goal is to show how two companies with different business strategies will make different decisions regarding the same suggested move, in a situation that every company encounters on a regular basis.

It is important to know that a company's business strategy can be changed, if necessary, and there are several ways to change it without causing excessive shocks, but we will not elaborate on this here.

Off-the-shelf product or tailor-made (customized) product

Another issue that is directly affected by a company's business strategy is the question of whether the company focuses on selling standard ("off-the-shelf") products, or products requiring adjustment ("tailor-made", or "customized" products) for each customer, or for some customers.

An off-the-shelf product is, as its name implies, a product that anyone can purchase at any time, and it is the same for all those who buy it. Whether it's granulated coffee, or invoice production software, or Microsoft 365 software, customers purchase these products as they are, without adjustment for the customer.

Products that require adjustment - there is a broad range in this category, from a product which undergoes minor changes to match customer requirements, to products that have been uniquely designed to specific customer requirements. There are (usually complex) products whose purpose is directly related to the work processes or methods of a particular organization, so it's necessary to adapt the product to the specific organization. Similarly, there are products that require integration into unique organizational systems, which in some cases will require the construction of dedicated interfaces per client.

There are, of course, many other examples, but the bottom line is that the difference between selling standard, off-the-shelf products, and selling products that need adjustment, are profound and significant, and must be taken into account. The differences between the two approaches are expressed, among other things, in the following areas:

A. Pricing

Off-the-shelf product pricing refers mainly to parameters that include:
- Market size, level of competitiveness.
- Product positioning, uniqueness.
- Cost of Goods Sold, which includes all elements related to the direct cost of the product, and in some cases also the cost of customer acquisition (we will discuss the issue in more detail below).
- Cost of product maintenance (ongoing improvements).
- Calculating the profit and loss of a product line that takes into account all the variables specified here and the level of profitability that the company aspires to and more…

Customized product pricing will typically include:
- Basic product cost, as mentioned above.
- Time and material for adaption i.e., how much time should be invested in the adaption process, plus the cost of materials if relevant.

B. Maintenance

For example, a software-based product usually releases a periodic version update (which includes bugs fixing, improved efficiency, added security, etc.). If the product is adapted to the customer, so that the result of the update is a different product variation for each customer, this has a complicating effect on the "build" or "compilation" process (the stage at which the software code of the new version is converted to an executable file that performs operations). That is, the build process must be executed separately for each customer. The larger implication of a separate product for each customer is that usually there is need for unique quality assurance tests per customer, a complex process that adds costs to the development and release processes.

C. Support

For a company that must provide support to a thousand customers who use the same product, it must organize its support process in a way which can be managed relatively simply – a certain number of people must be trained, all of whom need the same level of knowledge, and later on, this knowledge can also be transferred to a new employee, using the existing support team. On the other hand, the support of even only five customers, each of whom has a different product, is a complex activity, usually meaning massive investment in documentation. This makes the wait until an answer can be provided to every support request longer, because a support engineer needs time to review the documentation. Another option, or an additional one, is maintaining a separate dedicated support person for each customer, which depends, of course, on the product's value and complexity. Even pricing the support of a customized product can be more complex than pricing an off-the-shelf product, since it's composed of various combinations of pricing components, such as a fixed monthly payment plus an hourly component, an external expert, and more.

One territory or global activity

Is the company focused on one territory, or is it going to be global? The difference is significant in a large number of aspects. To demonstrate this, we will refer to a situation in which we aspire to be a global company:

How does global activity affect sales strategy?

1. Do you operate from one location, from the company headquarters, or set up sales offices in different territories? Or perhaps you start one way and move to the second way after meeting targets. Do you recruit employees in different territories, or do you use subcontractors?

2. Do you use distributors in some countries, not salespeople who are your own employees? If so, who manages the distributors? Are there countries that have both distributors and salespeople? How is the division between the two groups handled?

3. If employees are recruited, in most countries that means your local presence must be set up as a legal entity, and this has many, mainly operational, implications, and generates additional costs that must be taken into consideration.

4. Even if you decided not to establish sales offices in a certain country, but to manage sales from the company headquarters, when the volume of sales of tier1 customers exceeds several hundred thousand or millions of dollars, some customers will require that your company will have at the very least, a local

legal entity, and in some cases the customer will require the presence of a local support office.

5. Are your organization's IT systems designed for distributed deployment and maintenance?

6. The need for multi-currency support.

7. Organizational structure - There is a wide range of organizational structure options for an organization that operates globally, and each structure has advantages and disadvantages. Here are several options:

- All operations are concentrated and operated from the company headquarters, including operations in other territories. Activity in the framework of such a structure can succeed when the company is still small, or when is active in various countries through local distributors and cooperative agreements.

- Establishment of company offices in different territories (an office in one of the European countries, an office in Asia, etc.) Here too there are several possibilities:

    (a) A sales office.

    (b) An office with all that is required for full business activity, namely: salespeople, support, business development and marketing, finance, product management, and HR.

    (c) Any combination of option (a) and option (b) in different countries.

Options (b) and (c) produce additional complexity, which is in the domain of to whom do the local employees report, local management or the headquarters? Assuming that the office has a number of people, one of whom is defined as the office manager (or the site manager, or the chief executive officer of the territory) to whom do employees who provide company-wide functions that serve the territory, such as marketing, finance, or human resources, report? Do they report to the local manager (the territory manager) or to the manager in the company headquarters responsible for their service (the head of sales, the head of marketing, etc.)?

Each approach has advantages and disadvantages, so in many cases, we will see companies changing their organizational structure intermittently. Although there are several reasons for changing approaches, it is important to explain the main reason for the difficulty in deciding on the structure: the director of the local office responsible for business conduct in their territory needs the ability to manage all supporting functions that affect their success as a territory manager. The finance manager, for example, who should be the one to approve orders and contracts (including prices, payment terms, contract cancellation options, fines, indemnity for breach of contracts, etc.) will be the local office manager's chief assistant, so it makes sense that they report to the office manager. On the other hand, the legal and financial responsibility vis-à-vis the board of directors and shareholders is that of the head office, which includes the CFO (the chief financial officer), who sets the procedures that all regional financial managers must act according to. The CFO supervises all the regional financial officers, and is also the senior professional whom they should approach if there is a suspicion of contradictions or a failure to comply with the defined procedures. In order to make sure that everything is indeed done according to the CFO's instructions, and for direct financial control, it makes sense that the regional financial officers report to the CFO. These are two different perspectives, each will lead to a different conclusion; therefore, when you reach a decision point with regard to the organizational structure, it is important to get advice and weigh things in depth before making a decision.

Here, it should be noted that in very large organizations, there is a concept of "Solid Line Manager" and "Dotted Line Manager", to try to create a state in which one professional function has two managers, with a division in management.

But not only organization-wide functions can be problematic. For example, in working with a global customer that has activities in different countries around the world, who manages the customer? (a) One manager? (b) In any country in which the customer is active, the salesperson who is responsible for that country?

If one is managing the customer, where will they be located? Will they have to fly around and visit the same customer (or potential customer) in the many countries in which they have business activity, despite the fact that in those countries, the company may have a local salesperson who can perform this work and save quite a bit of expenses, not to mention that they are a speaker of the local language and know the local practices?

On the other hand, if each region's or country's salesperson manages the customer in that region or country, the question arises whether all managers in different regions must be coordinated in regards to the terms of the transactions, since information on prices, payment terms, support level, and other important transaction details in all regions will be available to all that customer's managers, and they will share this information with one another. So assuming that all sales managers in the different regions should indeed be coordinated for that global client, who is responsible for coordinating them?

How does global activity affect product adaption?

There are many parameters that are directly related to the product, or peripheral topics, that need to be taken into consideration; I will list some of them here:

1. Translation into different languages.

2. The name of a product developed in one country may have a negative connotation in another country.

3. Colors have different meanings in different countries.

4. Product size – an acceptable size in the US may be too large for the Japanese market.

5. Voltage and frequency of the power grid and cellular communication frequencies.

6. Local safety regulations or compliance with the country's standard.

7. Different measurement systems (metric vs. British/US).

8. Weather-resistance of your products (temperature, humidity, dust).

9. Software as a Service (SaaS). There are territories in which the quality and speed of the Internet are inadequate, which will prevent the use of software that requires very large data transfer by the cloud.

10. Tax and tariff issues - In some countries (e.g., Brazil), the taxation and tariffs for imports of hardware may reach up to 100%, a fact that could prevent the setting of a competitive price, mainly if there is a competitor that produces locally. Another example: if the company has subsidiary companies in different countries, but orders are also received from countries where the company does not have a local office, the company must check which local office (legal entity) it's better to issue invoices from. This is because there are various trade agreements between countries, and it is reasonable to assume that there are better trade conditions between one of the company's offices and the country the order was received from than there are in the other offices.

11. Regulation of data storage varies from country to country. The company must examine what measures must be taken to ensure the preservation of the information so that it will not leak (security regulations), and also check what information is allowed to be stored at all (privacy regulations).

12. Where the information is saved (where the servers are located): in different countries, there will be different requirements.

13. Customer support must be given in different languages, in accordance with the business activity. Here too, customer service can be implemented in several ways:

    ♦ The organization can build a support team that will include speakers of different languages.

    ♦ The organization may transfer this activity to a subcontractor, at least in all that relates to basic support (level 1/2), and then may build a separate team of a limited number of experts in support of complex problems (levels 3/4).

    ♦ If you are assisted by a subcontractor, here too there are two possibilities:

        ○ The contractor employs support personnel who speak the different languages.

        ○ The contractor employs support personnel who speak the languages in which there is significant business activity. For languages that are needed only rarely – the company will use a simultaneous translator when needed. This solution is usually significantly cheaper.

14. Companies whose product is hardware-based must build a logistical base for dealing with returns and repairs (RMA - Return Merchandise Authorization).

A device stops working, where do you send it for repair? There are quite a few options for logistical response, but the chosen operational system may sometimes be complex. The question "where do we send things?" is very simplistic – the answer may be complicated. I will raise points for the sake of general knowledge or for something to think about, without going too deeply into details.

There are industry-based hardware products that cannot be shipped for repair (or a major consumer product for a home, such as a refrigerator or an air conditioner).

Assuming that there is a service agreement, the options are:

- Ordering a technician from the company's representative office in that country.
- Flying company technicians in specially to solve the problem, especially in regards to unique equipment.

If the product can be sent for repair, the company must make shipping agreements, and then must decide where the product will be sent to:

- a service center in that country.
- a regional/continental service center.
- one main repair center.

A combination of these three options is actually a common solution, mainly because many types of equipment contain communication devices which have wireless or wired remote access over an internet network, allowing the support to characterize the fault remotely, and in accordance with the type of malfunction, to decide which repair center the product will be sent to.

Patent registration - yes or no?

Does the company try to protect its intellectual property with patents or not? I know of, and even acquired at a practically non-existent cost, companies in which patent registration became the main center of their activity. In practice, this distracted their focus, because most of the efforts and budgets that were supposed to be directed to the development of technology and products, and then marketing them, were diverted to just submitting dozens and hundreds of patent applications.

On the other hand, in one of the companies that I managed, we registered about seven patents, and one of them later saved us hundreds of thousands of dollars, and even more. How?

Start-up companies do not usually attract attention, but when they grow from sales of a few million dollars a year to tens and hundreds of millions of dollars a year, large competitors will take note of them and try different ways to delay the continuation of their growth, which will be mainly at their competitor's expense. One of the more common ways that big companies do this is to find cases of patent infringement, and file a claim. We must understand that this is not a simple procedure; that is, the plaintiff cannot capriciously submit a claim just because it seems to it that someone is infringing on a patent (at least according to the law in the United States); in order to file a claim, you need a reasonable level of evidence.

How did our patent save us money? When we began to bite deeply into a competitor's market share, we were served with a lawsuit for patent infringement. However, we were almost positive that they were in turn infringing on one of our patents. So once we were presented with the lawsuit, we relatively quickly arrived at an arrangement with our competitor that allowed us to use their patents, and in return we allowed them to use our patents. In my estimation, this arrangement allowed us to avoid legal battles that would have added up to hundreds of thousands of dollars and more.

The disadvantages of registering patents:

1. A long, uncertain process.

    It is very difficult to predict the chances of successful patent registration. For example, searching databases looking for similar patents isn't always a relevant and reliable way of ensuring that no competing patent hasn't already been applied for. You must remember that we are dealing with a process in which you receive your first response only between a few months and more than a year after you submitted your application for a patent (unless it is an accelerated process, which is more expensive), during which time no one examines the patent application; therefore, it is not possible to locate other patents submitted by various entities at the same time which possibly compete with the patent you submitted.

    Beyond that, nothing ensures that the patent application you submit will be accepted at the end. It may be that because of infringement on another existing patent, it will be necessary to shrink the patent application you submitted so much that its value will be limited merely to a declaratory advantage: "we have a patent," but the partial patent granted will not be something that will prevent, or even delay, others from developing a similar capability.

2. High costs – this depends on the number of patent applications and in which countries they are submitted, but over the course of a number of years, the cost of the patent attorney plus application fees plus the time the technical person spends on the patent application will reach a total of tens of thousands of dollars for one patent.

3. Lack of real value – out of the dozens of patent applications that I was connected to, only a few were blocking patents, ones which competitors would have to spend months of further development to detour around, and even after doing so, their solution wouldn't have been as good. In most cases, at least in the cases I encountered in 20 years, we ourselves succeeded, with a relatively small effort, to bypass patents; we made one change or other, and thus avoided being guilty of patent infringement.

4. Exposing technology – we must remember that in the application for patent registration, we expose the technology involved to the general public. Even if we do not reveal the fine details, the actual planning, information is still exposed, without any guarantee that the patent registration process will be successful. So there are quite a few cases, for example in the food industry, where it is better for the inventor to maintain their invention as a commercial secret, and not to expose it to the general public.

Advantages of registering patents:

1. A certain deterrence – especially when companies invest a lot of money developing technologies and products, registering a patent constitutes a deterrent against small and medium-sized competitors, who themselves are concerned about the costs of conducting legal proceedings.

2. Value added to the company - Patents constitute an additional layer in building the value of a company, and they are a parameter that venture capital financial firms tend to take into account when considering whether to invest in a company.

3. Formulating the idea of the product - the very process of writing the patent and investigating the presence of existing patents helps to formulate and refine the idea and/or product.

It should be remembered that there are many areas of activity, especially in software and applications, in which patent protection cannot be obtained.

So what was our reality in regards to business strategy?

Our executive team already discussed and defined each of the above issues during the course of the first two months, for, as I mentioned earlier, every decision in one of these issues has a broad and profound impact on all the organization's activities. The findings at the end of two months of investigation showed that there was a gap between the business strategy that the company thought it had, and the actual reality, with the emphasis on the following issues:

1. **Profitability or growth** – While in theory the company emphasized budgetary balance, actual performance showed that the opposite was happening. The main product was on a unique hardware platform, while new solutions emerging in the market were software-only based. Even though in our field there are a number of benefits to using a hardware platform, doing so also had obvious drawbacks.

   Software-only solutions have more flexibility in pricing mobility, and despite the fact that particularly the large customers were willing to pay a certain premium price for a better solution that includes dedicated hardware, software-only solutions "pulled" the price down. So in practice, price pressure bit into the profitability of the product compared to previous years.

   When we compared prices to a parallel period in previous years, we saw a sharp decline in the price we received for the hardware, and also a decline in the price of the software application sold as an add-on to the hardware. So there was a creeping and consistent decline in product profitability, while direct and indirect costs increased, **which effectively negated the chances of reaching a budgetary balance.**

How can we emerge from a state of deterioration in profitability, in a way which combines well with addressing the other problems that will be detailed below?

After reviewing the needs of the market (which we will elaborate on later), especially in looking at the three years ahead, we decided that the best option would be to develop a SaaS – Software as a Service – platform which would include most of our current functionality.

Our initial estimate of resources needed for the development of the Software as a Service platform was a year of development, and an additional investment of several million dollars. The new platform was planned to support 95% of our existing hardware platform's functionality, and also to provide a Software as a Service (SaaS) solution that meets several of the market demands that the software solutions that were recently released to the market failed to give a response to.

It was clear to us what technological challenges we would have to crack, and despite the fact that we identified them as high risks and challenges, we decided to take this risk.

The plan that was formulated assumed that at the end of the process we would meet the following objectives:

- A Software as a service (SaaS) solution that will enable 35% greater profitability compared to current profitability.
- Because we would have a software product that would be superior in quality to everything which is on the market, and which includes market-desired functionality, we could demand a price which is 7-10% higher than the price of competing solutions.

As soon as we had a SaaS solution, we planned to increase the price and profitability of our hardware solution by 30%; therefore, those customers who clearly preferred a hardware-based solution because of its unique benefits – especially with regard to information security – would be required to pay accordingly, so that even in regard to our hardware product, we defined a goal to significantly improve profitability.

It is important to examine how things evolved in terms of our 'growth or profitability' business strategy – the company's goal was first of all to achieve profitability.

After examining the issue, we came to the conclusion that based on the current product, our company will not be able to reach profitability. Some of the reasons have already been mentioned, and some further details will be provided below.

As a result of this conclusion, the company came to the conclusion that the most effective way to reach profitability was to invest in developing a new product, even if this will deepen the level of its short-term loss.

2. **An off-the-shelf product or a customized product.** Although the company thought it was producing an off-the-shelf product, the reality turned out to be the opposite.

In a detailed analysis, we found that about 70% of the total development resources were invested in adjusting the product to specific customer's needs.

The adjustments required were mostly minor, but because the software infrastructure was poor, any change became complex, and demanded endless regression testing. The result was both unacceptably low efficiency in utilizing development resources, and also disproportionate cost when it came to testing the product.

Our solution to this problem integrated well with solving problems in other issues. We began to formulate drastic measures, that were agreed to at executive management meetings, to cancel product adjustments, as we will describe in detail in the next chapter.

This is an excellent example of the importance of measuring parameters. For years, the company invested most of its development efforts in meeting customer requests for changes, and was dragged into a change-implementation spiral which further complicated the code and caused delays in making the changes, so that the vicious cycle became stronger and wider. The result: the increasing distance between the "off-the-shelf product" target and what actually occurred.

3. **One territory or a global company**. The organization had salespeople and support engineers in six different countries: the US, Brazil, Singapore, England, France, and Germany.

In terms of appropriateness to a business strategy that defined the company's activity as a global activity, with the goal of being number one in the world in terms of revenue and number of customers, this was a good match.

The next question was, whether it was right to spread ourselves over so many countries and continents? Was full global activity a good business strategy?

When our level of income from the various territories was examined, 90% of our income came from North America and Europe, with North America being more than 50% of revenues. Moreover, it seems that with the addition of new products that we will expand later on, there was fertile ground for a significant increase in these two territories down the road.

After my brief two-day visit to Singapore and two days in Brazil, and after a brief overview of business operations in Asia and South America, my conclusion was, as I explained in previous chapters, that there is no chance of selling our current products in both these regions at a reasonable profit and in significant quantities.

On the other hand, these are two areas that could be a significant growth engine for the company after we launch a series of new software products. Therefore, the question was asked whether it nevertheless would be worthwhile to maintain a smaller team in these regions for the purpose of building relationships with customers until we launched our new products, which was expected to be within a year.

What somewhat complicated the situation in South America was the agreement signed with one of the largest cellular operators in the region. The problem was that the agreement was problematic, and included conditions that in practice made the existing orders, and the orders that we hoped would arrive later, unprofitable. Nevertheless, I decided to leave the activity in Singapore and in South America in place, while reducing staff in both places.

In retrospect, my decisions about Brazil and Singapore were wrong. Yes, I reduced the costs somewhat, but after analyzing our activities in the area and identifying the low chance of success there in the coming years, the right thing to do would have been to cancel the agreement in South America, even if it involved fines of a million dollars, because it would have saved us operational costs of millions of dollars, and then to close operations in both South America and Singapore.

And even beyond that, there was a concern that in a company of our size, you can't accommodate the launch of a new product line in so many new territories at the same time. So the right thing to do would have been to restrict our activity to the two regions that generated 90% of our revenues: North America and Europe. Such a decision would have saved millions of dollars in two years, a sum that would have compensated us for our investment in the new product line, and would have brought us closer to the point of profitability.

4. **Patents Yes or No**. The company did not have a strategy on the matter.

Over the years, we filed only one patent, and this too had happened three years before. When the new executive team examined this subject at the outset of its activities, we decided that in a quarterly review of the subjects treated by the research group, we'll apply for a patent for any research that leads us a to breakthrough. Indeed, over the next nearly two years, we submitted applications for three additional patents.

Establishing vision and growth engines

After 100 days had passed since I started on the job, and after I established the management team, we gathered for two days at an offsite. This was the first time we had gathered together as an executive team. Most of us had only recently joined the team, so I set three goals for the meeting:

1. Introducing the management team and forming a team spirit.
2. Formulating our business strategy.
3. Making decisions regarding our product line for the next 18 months.

We decided in advance that the organization's business goals for 2017 will be discussed at a later stage towards the end of 2016.

Strategies in regards to market, customers, products and our company

We defined a number of topics for discussion which would lead us to formulate the vision:

1. **Market size**
    - What is our market?

- What is the size of the market that we can serve (Serviceable Addressable Market)?
- Is our market growing or decreasing?
- What is our current market share, and has it grown or decreased over the last two-three years?

2. **Customers**
    - Who are our customers, and whom do we think should be our customers, but they aren't?
    - What is the business model of our customers – how do they profit from our products/services?
    - What is the money flow path for the services provided by our products?
    - Do we have a way to influence the flow of money? Does the current path create more opportunities for us?

3. **Products**
    - What is the level of readiness of products that we launch?
    - Are all products necessary? Can we cancel some of them?
    - How does performance compare to specifications?
    - Usability level.

4. **Our company**
    - Our current market positioning.
    - What we would like our positioning to be, and how can we bridge the gap?
    - Our current positioning, as our employees see it.
    - What we would like our positioning to be, and how can we bridge the gap?

What are our market size and share?

What is our market? This first and fundamental question gave rise to a long and stormy debate.

Over the years, our company's basic market was retail chains which sell, among other things, cellphones. There are several types of such stores:

- Chain stores owned by the cellular operators.
- Cellular operators franchise stores.
- General retail chains such as Bestbuy, Walmart, and others.
- Stores that fix phones.

Recently, our company also considered entering the After Market Services (AMS) market which includes:

- Stores that buy and sell second-hand cellphones (Buyback).
- Stores that refurbish second-hand cellphones (Refurbish).
- Insurance companies that insure cellphones.

When we examined the market, we decided to separate the market of retail chains which sell phones, which we have experience in and that we understand well, and the AMS market, which was new to us.

The market of retail chains which sell phones

We reached a number of conclusions regarding market size:

1. The size of our general market is the number of cellphones sold, and this market grew by 3% per year.

   For example, the number of phones sold in 2016 in North America was about 200 million. However:

2. Is our relevant target market growing or decreasing? Our current product is hardware-based, and used in stores. Phone sales in retail stores are down on average by about 4% a year, while online purchases are growing by about 7% a year.

   When the whole picture is put together, it turned out that **our market, limited to stores, is decreasing annually by 4%.**

3. What is our market share and is it growing or decreasing?

   From a market survey conducted in advance in the countries that we are active in, we learned that our service is relevant only to 50% of those who buy phones in stores. At the same time, we also discovered that our services are relevant to 25% of those who buy online and are willing to go to the store to get our service.

   When we compared these numbers to the number of transactions our products perform, we found that our market share in North America, when we relate to providing service in stores, is 20% smaller than we thought. However, when we examined the data of previous years in North America, there was no indication of a change in our market share relative to our competitors.

   On the other hand, we did see a reduction in our market share in Europe. What is the difference between the markets, why was there a decrease in Europe and stability in North America?

   The reason is mainly related to the type of customers in the two markets (as will be explained below) and new competitors who offered a software-based solution (I will expand on this below too).

   Regarding our market share outside a store, i.e. on the move or at home, where the demand is growing, our market share is zero, because we don't have software products that can be used outside a store.

The first conclusion – what we had already hypothesized had been definitively verified after the numbers were presented – to bring about a real change, we must divert resources to develop a Software as a Service (SaaS) solution. The question remains – where do we divert resources from?

The AMS market

We reached a number of observations regarding market size:

1. The parameter defining the size of the AMS market is the number of second-hand phones sold (Buyback), and this market grew by 22% per year, and is planned to continue growing at this rate over the next five years.

   For example, the number of second-hand phones sold worldwide in 2016 was about 120 million.

   What is the significance of the 120 million second-hand phones sold every year?

   There are several:

   - It takes 120 million tests to determine the value of these phones, one for each phone. This test can be done at a store or remotely; the average price today in the market for this test is one dollar, that is, a total market of $120 million.

   - After the seller and the store or the buying business agree on the sale, the buying business (Buyback Vendor) sends the phone to a renovation center, and there, too, 120 million tests are needed. The average price for testing is also one dollar, which means a total market of 120 million dollars.

   - After the test, all owner information is erased from the original phone, so that it doesn't pass on to the new buyer. There are several levels of erasing information, and cost will range from 20 cents to one dollar each, which means an additional market of $24-120 million.

♦ Summing up all these actions indicates that the total business opportunity in 2016 of the AMS market was $264-360 million, and it grew by 22% per year.

Since all indicators show that the market is just getting started, we estimated there would be price erosion over time, and still, this is a very large market.

2. What is our market share? – Currently, zero.

Although some **tests to determine the phone's value** are carried out in the store, our buyback testing function wasn't of high enough quality at this point in time.

We didn't have a well-prepared product for the renovation centers, so our market share there is also currently zero.

The AMS session's conclusion – the AMS market is growing at a significantly faster pace than the retail market that we operate in. We also have many technological components that are appropriate for this market, but we don't have enough products, expertise, and experience in this field.

Who are our customers and what is their business model?

Our customers should also be divided into two groups:
- Retail chains which sell phones.
- The AMS market – companies that buy used phones and companies which renovate used phones.

Customers – retail chains that sell phones

1. As we have already shown, we can categorize the retail chains that sell cellphones to four types according to their business model:

    a. Cellular operators' stores – In the United States, there are about 15,000 such stores.

    b. Franchise stores of cellular operators – The US has about 10,000 such stores.

    c. Retail chains – There are approximately 2,000 relevant stores in the US.

    d. Stores that focus on cellphone repair – There are about 5,000 such stores in the United States.

    Of the four categories, almost all of our sales were in category (a), cellular operators' stores.

    It is very important to understand why we succeed in just one category.

    The lack of access to the other categories limits our ability to grow in the market of the other stores, which itself is also a shrinking market.

2. What is the business model for each category?

    ◆ **Cellular operators' stores** are the most significant component of our total customers, as of the end of 2016.

    What motivates cellular companies to sell phones is mainly the opportunity it presents to lock customers into their cellular network. Spreading payments for the purchase of a new phone over 36 months, for example, definitely creates a strong connection between the customer and the cellular company, since the payments for the phone are included in the bill for the cellular services. The use of our products enables data transfer immediately from the old cellphone to the new one, which means the customer can be out of the store door ten minutes after buying the new cellphone. That means fast service and a satisfied customer, who purchased a new cellphone on convenient installments, and these same installments guarantee that the customer will continue to use the operator's network. This is the business model.

Of course, the profit on selling the phone is also part of the model, though it's a small fraction compared to locking the customer into using the operator's network.

- **The cellular operators' franchise stores** – for these stores, the most significant profit is by the sale of the phone. Therefore, unlike the stores owned by the cellular operator, in which the calculation of profit also includes income from continued monthly use of their cellular network, the franchise store's profit margin is much smaller. Therefore, their sensitivity to the price of equipment like ours is much greater. Their price for the phone is limited from above by what customers are willing to pay, as determined by other competitive retail stores. On the other hand, their price is limited from below by the phone's cost, as determined by its manufacturer.

- Retail chains – a model very similar to franchise stores, with two differences:
  - Retail chains work on the assumption that people who buy phones in their stores also purchase additional electronic items there, not necessarily related to cellphones.
  - We noticed a behavioral change: more retail stores, mostly in Europe, are demanding payment for the

service provided by our equipment. It turns out that the payment is usually between $10-20. We also see that this practice is quite common in the Scandinavian countries, and is in the initial stages of adoption in other European countries.

In light of this information – charging the customer for our services – we decided to carry out a small experiment that took place several weeks after the executive team's first meeting. In an experiment conducted together with a potential customer, the customers who purchased a phone were offered an option to transfer the information from the old phone to the new one with the help of our equipment. The experiment lasted three weeks; during the first week the service was offered for free, in the second week, customers were required to pay $10 for the service, and in the third week, customers were required to pay $20 for the service. We, along with the retail management, wanted to test if there is a change in demand for the service following the change in price.

To our great surprise, and to the surprise of the retail customer, no behavioral change occurred when the price changed. In other words, the ratio between the people who asked for the service and the total phone buyers was the same in the three cases.

When we analyzed why this was, we came to the conclusion that a customer who paid $300-$700 for a new phone won't hesitate to pay a few more dollars so that the contents of their old phone will be transferred to the new phone, so that it can be used within a few minutes.

However, the very fact that we couldn't change the behavior of retailers was interesting. That is, we used the experiment's data to try to convince other retailers to charge money for our service. What we found was that as long as some retailers charge for our service, their competitors feel comfortable charging too, but if the market doesn't charge money, no one wants to be the first to do so.

- **Stores who focus on repairing cellphones** – this is a growing market. The longer the life of cellphones - second-hand phones market grows –the greater the number of these stores. The domain is still new, and from the little interaction we had so far with stores of this kind, it turned out that they were interested in a Software as a Service (SaaS) solution, where the most important parameter is the need to evaluate the battery's condition. We will discuss this later.

    However, there is another aspect that has become of utmost importance to understanding the market – phones that are under warranty, that is phones that were purchased new and have a one-or-two-year warranty. What happens when there is a problem with these phones? In most cases, the customer returns to the store they bought the phone, which normally sends the phone for repair. The manufacturer usually bears the cost of sending the phone for repair and repairing it, apart from a situation in which the same store or retail network sends many phones for repair, and it turns out they aren't defective. In such a situation, the manufacturer will charge the retail network for some of the expense of dealing with the phone, so stores have an interest not to send a phone for repair before they make sure there is a problem with it.

That is, when we refer to stores that focus on repairing phones, there are actually two different types:

- Those that handle phones that are not under warranty.
- Those who sold the phone and now are "forced" to take care of it as long as the phone is under warranty. The business model in these cases is to invest a little time in checking whether the phone works properly or not, and try to make an up-sale, i.e. to take advantage of the opportunity that the customer is in the store again to sell more items, or maybe to upgrade their phone to a newer model.

We get into this picture when it comes to testing the phone quickly, with our diagnostic product that enables diagnosing the phone's condition in a few minutes, and in most cases, if the problem is related to software or a virus, even to fix it. And again – it is important to mention that sending a functional phone for repair costs the retail network money. To our great surprise, the use of our diagnostic product was low, and at this stage, **we had no well-founded explanation** as to why this was. We will return to the analysis of the reasons for this when we discuss the usability level of our products.

Customers from the After Market Services (AMS) market

This group is divided into three types of customers:

1. Customers that buy second-hand phones (Buyback).
2. Customers that refurbish.
3. Insurance companies.

We focused on second-hand phone buyers and customers that refurbish phones. At this stage, we didn't know enough about the insurance companies.

What is these companies' business model?

1. Companies which buy second-hand phones (Buyback vendors) – As previously described, retail chains strive to sell as large a number of new phones as possible. In some cases, they promote sales of new phones by way of trade-in sales. But dealing with all the used phones the retail chains "bought", which the retail chains have no use for, is done by companies designed just for this – the Buyback companies.

   There are two main types of activity of companies of this type:

   ◆ A Buyback company and the retail chain agree in advance on a price for the various models, without checking the phones. In effect, the Buyback company buys the entire inventory of used phones purchased by the retail chain as part of a trade-in plan.

   A large portion of the purchased phones will be transferred to emerging markets overseas, where the prices of new phones are higher, and therefore a second-hand market is flourishing. So you can see a movement that starts in the US, for example, where the used phones are sent to be sold in Asian countries.

   ◆ According to a model that was used only to a limited extent (but as of 2016, there was a desire to make it standard and automatic): the cellphones are checked in the store, and a price can be set there on the spot by a representative of the Buyback company, with a percentage of the price going to the retailer. The advantage of this model is – the price that is determined accurately represents, on the face of it, the phone's condition. "On the face of it," because at the time, the tools for full automation of examining all of the phone's functions were limited. However, it was still possible to check relatively quickly the important elements which determine the phone's value, including external appearance and screen condition (including touch screen), and to check if it is stolen.

There were two main reasons why the model was implemented only partially:

- An employee would have to be in the store to perform the test and manage the process, which made the process very expensive.
- Not much functionality could have been tested in the retail store, and defects were discovered in quite a few of the phones that came to the Buyback company for a complete inspection and renewal, which lead to a loss.

We identified an opportunity for us here, if we could fully automate the process, namely:

- A second-hand phone that comes for testing connects to our equipment, which checks all parameters.
- The results are transmitted to an automated calculation engine of the buyback company.
- The price is returned completely automatically to the phone in real time.
- The price is displayed on the phone screen and all this process takes no more than a few minutes – there's an interesting business opportunity here.

♦ There is another business model, which currently represents a small market, but one that is gaining momentum, and a significant increase is expected in the following years. These are small Buyback companies, all of whose activity is carried out online only. They buy second-hand phones and sell them through a number of channels: through their website or through other sites, including Amazon. Their challenge is to precisely evaluate the phone's condition before they purchase it through an entirely online process.

Because technology hadn't yet fully enabled this (technology which enabled inspecting the screen's quality online wasn't available in 2016), they used an integrated method, according to which:

- The seller fills out a questionnaire.
- Depending on the answers, the price appears with a disclaimer: if, after the phone arrives for inspection, the buyer discovers a difference between the actual condition of the phone and what is specified in the questionnaire, the buyer has the right to offer a different price.
- If such a difference is indeed found, the seller is contacted and offered an updated price.
- If the seller agrees to the updated price, the money is paid, and the process is over. If they don't agree, the buyer returns the phone to the seller.

This process itself is rather cumbersome, especially because, on the one hand, in more than 25% of the phones, there is a difference between what was reported on the questionnaire and the actual condition, it is therefore difficult to significantly expand (scaleup) the business activity according to this model. On the other hand, there is again a business opportunity here for us, if we launch a suitable product which does enable remotely checking all the parameters, including the screen.

2. **Companies that renew cellphones (Refurbish)**

   Once used phones are purchased, they are sent for refurbishing. The meaning of refurbishing is:

   - Erasing existing information on the phone. The quality of the erasure is determined according to the regulation of that country, or the destination country which the phones are sent to. It is important to note that there are different levels of erasure, and in most cases, data can nevertheless be recovered (as of 2018).
   - A thorough check of the phone, including all internal functions.
   - Repairing the phone if a problem is detected, or disqualifying and rejecting the phone if repair isn't possible or not worthwhile.
   - Final inspection after repair.
   - Loading applications as per the final customer's request – this is still performed in a small percentage of cases.

   To perform these activities effectively, especially because our potential customers inspect hundreds of thousands to millions of phones per year, the inspection should be done in parallel on a large number of phones. In other words, in order for a product to be relevant to this market, it should be able to operate the phone completely automatically from the moment a cable connects to the phone, and should issue an alert about malfunctions. The product should be able to do this quickly, in no more than minutes, and the product must run at the same time on dozens of phones. All this in parallel to being able to identify as many cellphone models as possible, of which there are many thousands.

From conversations we had with several companies, we could detect business structure change in this market. If, at the beginning, there was a separation between Buyback and Refurbish companies, we now see more companies are performing these two functions. In fact, in practice, it seems that more and more medium and large companies, those who buy between tens of thousands and millions of phones a year, provide both services in order to streamline processes and reduce costs.

In other words, the companies that have both functions, manage, as far as they are concerned, two interface points:

(a) with the retail stores who request that they purchase the phones of customers performing a trade-in.

(b) with the companies they want to sell the refurbished phones to. This involves operational work that needs to be done efficiently, because the profit margins of this entire operation are quite low. From some inquiries, we understood that the operating profit is only a few percent.

Reviewing our products

It was important to review the following topics:

1. What is the level of readiness of the products we are launching?
2. Are all our products necessary? Can we cancel some of them?
3. The products' performance level.
4. The products' usability level.

   This discussion's goal was to understand what the problems with our current products are. A good way to do this is to ask each of the participants to rank, in order of importance, five limitations or disadvantages of our product lines. The next step was to hear what the customers thought about us and our products, and to see the matching level on the different parameters.

What is the readiness level of products that we launch, and how can we improve?

The reactions of most of the staff were similar. When we launch a product or a new feature, it is released to the market at a low level of readiness. This is especially reflected in the number of bugs recorded by customers, bugs which in too high a percentage of cases, prevent the customer from using the product or the feature.

Other important feedback indicated that the development and QA teams react quickly to critical bugs, so that within a few weeks the product actually enters a reasonable quality work mode. This clearly indicates the need to improve product release procedures. The problems identified went beyond insufficient stability and bugs, and included peripheral themes such as release notes, sales engineer training, translation to supported languages, and so on.

This issue was subsequently addressed as a top priority, and over the next few months, our company achieved significant improvement through a wide range of steps, some of which I will list:

1. It was decided to upload a testing server on the cloud to enable customers and employees to test our products and new capabilities and deliver feedback and comments before releasing a production version.

2. It was decided to change the development structure and the development processes, as will be detailed below. The goal was, among other things, to move up the testing phase, so that it will be carried out concurrently with development.

3. It turned out that in some cases, features tested in the country the R&D was located and found working properly, don't work in some other countries. Therefore, it was decided later on to perform Crowd Testing; there are a number of companies that provide this service, which allows testing by the user community in different countries, using a wide range of phones and local networks.

4. It was decided to establish a dedicated team for automated testing, and to measure our increase rate in automated tests usage.

Are all of our products necessary? Can we cancel some of them?

Before we started the discussion on these products to be developed in the next 18 months, it was important to discuss if there are products that we can cancel.

A discussion about eliminating products is always important, emotional and complex.

This is an important discussion because any product to be canceled, releases R&D capacity that can be diverted to more profitable products. Similarly, the time and attention devoted to the canceled product by the entire organization are also released. On the other hand, canceling a product may reduce revenue, if there is no product to replace it in the market niche it serves.

In general, a discussion about canceling products is usually difficult; there will always be those who will claim the product is important, that customers ask for it, and it is of strategic importance for various reasons. They may be right, but a discussion about product life must nevertheless be carried out regularly, once a quarter or once a year, and we took advantage of this opportunity that presented itself in the off-site meeting to have an initial discussion of this subject.

The bottom line is that we have to analyze the situation on the basis of several parameters:

- Which market does a specific product open up that we can't fulfill with another existing product?
- Expected earnings/profit of the product.
- Product maintenance. It's true that this is on the face of it included in the products' profit and loss calculations, but this isn't enough. I'll give an example. Our company has developed software on several platforms. Many capabilities were available on multiple platforms, but the code for each of them was written differently, so if a correction in a certain capability was made, the code change was different depending on each platform, which demanded duplicate work, according to the number of platforms, instead of making the change only one time.

It was decided to take advantage of the opportunity to seriously consider the possibility of merging all platforms, so that a change made in one place would be executed automatically in the others. This meant that there was a need to rewrite code, and the broader meaning was to stop supporting products until the merging process was fully carried out.

Following this discussion, we reached the conclusion that we have to give up several products:

- We had three different hardware platforms, and we decided that two platforms could cover all market requirements, so we decided to cancel one product line.

- We had an old line of application products that, in the opinion of many of our staff, didn't meet current UI/UX standards and it was decided to stop any investment in it.

- Software as a service (SaaS) platform for customer service – when there is problem with a cellphone, the user usually calls the cellular company or the company from which it purchased the phone. These companies usually employ a subcontractor which has a customer support center, who will try to provide a solution. In the case of a cellphone, it is difficult to be very responsive when the phone isn't working. We had a solution that enabled us to perform remote testing and in most cases to remotely solve the problem, but it was not perfect, and we didn't know enough about this business segment and its ecosystem. Therefore, we decided that without a full understanding of this specific business area, we would stop the development and marketing of this product line.

Bottom Line – During a few efficient and practical hours, we stopped the development of, or canceled, nearly 50% of our company's products.

Product performance level

How do we measure product performance? We looked at the following parameters:

1. **How well do we comply with the product's specification?** – On the basis of a preliminary review, we could conclude that from a functional point of view, there is a high degree of

compatibility between the product datasheet and the actual situation.

2. **Parameters that don't appear in the specification, compared to what we think should serve as a quality threshold** – that is, given the information we have today about parameters we wouldn't necessarily mention in the specification but which we would like to track differently, we identified the following parameters:

- The number of bugs – this was a parameter that hadn't been measured so far in a way that enabled drawing vital information, but for us, it was a critical point. We decided on two levels of activity:
  - To define four levels of bugs: Minor, Major, Critical, Blocker, for each of which we must provide a clear definition.
  - It was also decided to measure the bugs that are the result of regression.
  - The last thing – for any bug (Major, Critical, Blocker reported by a customer), we must specify in the (RCA – Root Cause Analysis) report how it happened and how to prevent it in the future.

- Product activity accuracy – We identified inaccuracies in several parameters which require correction. Even in this case, there is no precise definition of the accuracy of tests or features. We didn't find that our competitors had such a parameter either. We decided to make a change, marking the five most important tests, and define a target for their accuracy.

- Successful run end percentage – This is the percentage of runs that end successfully, out of all the activations of our products that a customer runs in the store. We detected a great difference between runs of certain activities versus others, but we couldn't explain or analyze the results, meaning we couldn't identify what the reasons for this or that percentage are.

In this case too, neither we nor our competitors had a precise definition of the percentage of runs that end successfully.

It is important to understand that there is a large variety of reasons that the run didn't end successfully. It could be because of a bug, it could be that the customer changed their mind and hit Abort, and it could also be that at a certain stage of the action, the operator was required to choose between alternative options, and they didn't respond.

Despite all this, we decided to set up a small team to define which logs had to be put into the system to enable us to analyze the reasons for a run not to end successfully, and to improve the result. We should say up-front that this process of analysis and improvement, from beginning to end, that is, until we could define goals and meet them, took about a year.

3. **Where do we stand compared with competitors' solutions?** There were several parameters which we had a significant advantage in, and there were some in which we at a disadvantage. I will address the main parameters, that aren't always directly related to the product.

    ♦ Our parent company was very successful in its market, with an excellent brand in regards to both the product aspect and the aspect of financial strength, and that was in our favor. At this point, our customers were mostly leading retail chains, customers for whom the financial stability of their suppliers is a major criterion, and here we had an advantage over the other players in the market.

- Our main platform was a hardware platform; in regards to information security, it was unique. Information transfer was performed directly between the phones, so no information is stored externally in the course of the transfer. This is in comparison to other existing solutions, which left remnants of information that could be restored with a particular effort. For some customers, mainly cellular operators – whose retail division was our biggest customer – this is a very important issue.

It is important to understand that according to the regulator, cellular operators are considered Data Controllers. By law, they are the ones who will pay the price in case of theft of private user information. We, and companies like us, are considered Data Processors, that is, a type of sub-contractor who is asked to do something with the private information of a user, but if this information is stolen, the Data Controller, which is our customer, will pay most of the price. That's why there is such sensitivity to protecting user data.

Before we go further, we will expand on this important issue.

Data Controller or Data Processor, according to GDPR

Let's begin by defining the concept of GDPR, as listed in Wikipedia:

> **GDPR – General Data Protection Regulation** *"is a collection of mandatory instructions that have been regulated by the European Parliament, the Council of the European Union, and the European Commission, in order to protect the topics of information in the European Union's territory in all that relates to the processing of their citizens' personal data. This regulation refers to the collection, retention, and transfer of personal data of individuals, and establishes uniform rules for privacy. The regulation is mainly intended to allow every resident of the EU maximum control over the details that were kept about them in private, public and business and government companies, by applying enforceable legal rules to those entities."*

According to the GDPR, organizations must understand the difference between a data controller and a data processor.

Depending on an organization's definition by this division, the GDPR determines duties and limitations on what the organization can do with users' personal data and who is responsible for what.

What is a Data Controller?

A Data Controller is a central entity when it comes to protecting the rights of data owners.

A Data Controller, as its name implies, controls the overall purpose and the means, or 'why' and 'how' to use the data.

A Data Controller can also process the data according to its means. There may be situations where a Data Controller should use an external service to process the data (a company like us).

In this case, the Data Controller allows another company (for example, us) to process the personal data of users. This doesn't mean that the Data Controller gives "control" to another company. The Data Controller remains in control by defining for the company that processes the data, what exactly it is allowed to process and do with the information.

These situations are increasingly common in today's economy. That is why we must clarify the Data Processor's role.

What is a Data Processor?

As we have seen, the Data Controller can use an external organization to process the data under its control. Organizations that process data on behalf of Data Controllers are called Data Processors.

It is important to note that the Data Processor doesn't control the data, and cannot change the purpose or use of the particular data set. The Data Processor is limited to data processing in accordance with the instructions and purpose provided by the Data Controller. A good way to think about the Data Processor is as a special technical partner, who is appointed to perform specific tasks to achieve the goals set by the Data Controller.

Why is this distinction important?

In a perfect world, both the Data Controller and the Data Processor know their respective roles exactly, and communication between them is excellent. Unfortunately, the real world is far from perfect, and therefore the GDPR determines a framework and functions in case problems arise.

A common example in which awareness of the role of the Data Controller and the Data Processor is critical is theft of the user data. In this case, the companies involved must ensure that they all have acted in accordance with the limitations of their liability.

Okay, so what?

In today's business world, it is important to understand that almost every Data Controller outsources some of the data processing to an external Data Processor. The Data Controller must verify that the different Data Processors working with them are aware of their obligations according to the GDPR.

Our recommendation, that is at a level of a mutual obligation: make sure that there is a clear and specific data processing agreement before the Data Controller delivers any work to the Data Processor. An agreement that defines the role and limits of what is permitted to the Data Processor is equally important to both parties.

It's important to know what the involvement of your company is in regards to the specific data that you are dealing with.

How do I know if I am a Data Controller or a Data Processor?

As in many areas of our lives, things aren't always black and white. In some cases, there may be gray areas, and you may need expert advice to clarify your category.

Here's a quick guide to help you understand your role when handling personal data.

You may be the Data Controller if your organization decides:

- To collect personal data according to a legal basis that allows it to do this;
- Which items of personal data to collect;
- To change the data;
- The purpose or purposes for which the data are used;

- Whether to share the data, and if so, with whom;
- How long to save the data.

Your organization may be a Data Processor if it is guided by the Data Controller to perform some of the following tasks:

- Implement IT systems or other methods of collecting personal data.
- Use certain tools or techniques to collect personal data.
- Install security around the personal data.
- Store the personal data.
- Transfer the personal data from one organization to another.

This list is incomplete and there may sometimes be uncertainty about the distinction between a Data Controller and a Data Processor. If a company has doubts about which category it's in, it is always advised to consult a legal expert on the subject.

The product usability level

We will now return to the state of our products at this time – now is the time to analyze the subject of our products' usability level.

1. **The usability level** – in my opinion, this is the most important parameter.

   The usability level and usage trend combine two indicators:
   - How needed is the product?
   - Is it useable?

   In the end, we want the customer to renew its license or purchase the next version, and will only do so if:

   (a) they feel a need for the product's capabilities.

   (b) the product is efficient and simple to use.

Building a financial plan for the next year is the basis for any future business activity of a company. In order for us to accurately construct such a plan, being able to predict the percentage of license renewals next year is critical, otherwise, our financial plan's accuracy will be low, in addition to the fact that the profitability of renewing licenses is relatively high. It's worth devoting a minute to think about this:

When it comes to renewing licenses, we're usually referring to software, where the profit margin will be high. In license renewal, there is no process of introducing the product to a new customer with all the investment that relates to it, which means the sale cost is relatively low. The time required to sell license renewal is much shorter than the time required for a new sale, since there are usually no negotiations about the terms or the price, because the contract already exists. No matter how we look at it, renewing licenses is much more profitable than acquiring a new customer.

To understand this, you must understand who the end customer is.

When we refer to retail chains, we mean two layers of customers: The first layer consists of store managers and the operators in the stores, who are the ones who "feel" the product and the value which it produces for them, since they serve their customers. They are also those that decide how much to use the product.

The second layer is the senior managers, who are measured mainly according to general business parameters, such as the level of income in stores or the number of phones that are sold in installments, or parameters that enable predicting the business future, like the Net Promoter Score (NPS) – we'll explain what this measure is later on. If so, we must be aware that despite the fact that the final decision is in the hands of senior management, before the senior officials make a decision they will consult with the store managers and ask for their opinion, so the product must meet the needs of both levels.

In terms of usability level, although the level of information was limited, we could detect some interesting data.

The product that enables data transfer from an old cellphone to a new one:

1. At the level of total use, we saw a decrease of a few percent in use of this product each year. The explanation for this was given in a previous chapter dealing with "the market of retail chains that sell phones" – where we explained that this decrease is due to the increase in purchasing phones online, at the expense of purchasing them in stores.

2. There was a difference in use between stores. We could see a correlation between stores which updated software for advanced versions and usage level. New versions also included bug fixing and updates for support of new cellphones. That is, if you didn't download the latest version of the product, it could be that it won't support a new phone that has just been launched, so you can't transfer information to it from an old phone, which will reduce the usability level.

3. There was also a difference in use level between small and large stores in the same chain. Our initial and not well-founded explanation for this difference was that in most of the stores, the salespeople are very young, and their turnover rate is high. In a small store, there may be only one or two employees, and in general, only one of them knows how to operate the product, so if that employee leaves, knowledge about the product may possibly not be transferred, so that use of the product stops.

In contrast, in large stores, where there will be a number of our products, even if one operator leaves, there will always be another employee who can explain to their replacement what our product does and how to operate it.

The product which diagnoses cellphones and resolves software problems:

This is a relatively new product launched at the end of 2015 and sold mainly in Europe and a bit in North America. The level of use in general was very low, in relation to the level of need that the customers emphasized to us.

However, we could see one customer whose level of use was high beyond any expectation. We had no explanation for the profound difference between most customers and this unique customer. It took us a lot of field work until we understood what would define the level of usability. We'll describe the factors in detail when we discuss in the topic of Customer Success in the chapter "**Building an infrastructure for growth**."

The discussion's result – we approved a request to establish a Customer Success function whose purpose is:

1. To define parameters for usability level
2. To investigate in depth the reasons for different usage levels
3. To make recommendations for increasing the level of use, by type of customer and type of product
4. To adopt a platform that identifies a low level of usability, warns the customer and its account manager, and helps the customer improve it.

We decided that Yoni Danieli, VP of Quality, would be responsible for this area.

What customers think of us and the NPS (Net Promoter Score) index

It was important for us to understand what customers think of us on several issues, and to measure ourselves according to the NPS index. What is this measure?

The Net Promoter Score Index (NPS) is intended to represent the degree of customer loyalty to the company or product. This index is based on a survey of one question, which was found to be most reliable in representing and predicting customer behavior. The answer is from 0 to 10.

The question is: **"To what extent would you recommend the product/service/company to a friend or colleague?"**

The use of this index is very common worldwide, and allows companies to examine and compare their score to that of competing companies in the same industry. One of the conclusions of the study that gave rise to this measure is that "satisfaction surveys" don't really reflect customer behavior, and therefore aren't very effective.

On the other hand, the willingness of customers to recommend a product/ service/company to friends and acquaintances is a reliable indication of satisfaction, since by making a personal recommendation they also "take a risk", by virtue of the fact that the recommendation is "personal," which is a sign of high loyalty. Therefore, the index also constitutes a tool for forecasting growth in the company's customer base.

Many studies have shown that the index results are correlated with future business growth. That is, if there was an improvement in the score relative to the previous measurement, this is likely to be reflected in an increase in future income levels.

Hence, if you are looking for a more scientific way to

understand the power of your brand than relying on internet online reviews, NPS is a simple and effective measure to use. One of NPS' great advantages is the possibility of evaluating your company's results against competitors.

Calculating the NPS score

I'll be using product as the item we are evaluating, and as indicated before, you can replace it with service or company.

Customers should rate the product following the NPS question on a scale of 0-10

Once you have the results, you need to categorize them into three categories and calculate each of them as a percentage from the overall number of responses: and after that its really simple, so:

First category - **Detractors** - Anyone who scores 6 or below is considered a Detractor. Those are not particularly thrilled by the product.

Second category – are the **Passives** - Anyone who scores 7-8 is considered passive.

And the third category – are the **Promoters** - anyone who scores 9 or 10 is considered a promoter.

NPS = (number of Promoters - number of Detractors) / (number of responses) x 100 to get the number in %. In other words, and maybe in a simpler form, the **NPS = the number of Promoters in % - number of Detractors in %.**

Let's use the following Example: 100 customers responses were received:

10 responses were in the range of 0-6 (Detractors) - 10%

20 responses were in the range 7-8 (Passives) - 20%

70 responses were in the range 9-10 (Promoters) - 70%

To calculate the NPS score, 10% (Detractors) should be deducted from 70% (Promoters), which equal 60%. The score is always shown only as an integer, so the NPS result in this case is simply 60. The NPS score can also be negative and it ranges from -100 to +100.

Survey results

Within our customer's organization, at whom should we target this survey?

The survey with the NPS question, should target those who decide how much to use your products if at all, meaning the end customers – those that are using the product and who are directly exposed to its advantages and disadvantages. Large customers have several layers of decision makers: from users, to IT, procurement, finance and then management, but the most important ones are the end users, those who without their recommendation, you will have a hard time selling or renewing licenses.

It is important to note that this was the first time that we calculated the NPS index, and thus we had no indication of our situation as compared to previous years. However, we could compare the results from North America to those from Europe, and indeed, there was a fundamental difference.

While the NPS results in North America were positive, i.e. more customers would recommend us compared to those who criticize us, the situation in Europe was different. When we analyzed the results, the conclusions in regards to the differences were very interesting, and enabled us to formulate measures for improvement:

- One of the most prominent parameters that we received criticism about is customer support. The criticism was greater when the language in question wasn't English. When we looked at our support system, most of the employees were indeed English-speakers, because most of our customers were English speakers.

    The level of backup in other languages was smaller, so there was a greater chance of slipups. For example, a German-speaking employee who didn't come to work produces a more significant hole than an English-speaking employee who would be absent that day. When we later analyzed our response time to questions in different languages, we have indeed seen a difference, i.e. it took a longer time to respond to non-English speakers, which made them less satisfied.

- Other complaints were about product stability (number of bugs). Here, the result is related to how we operate in Europe relative to North America. Our diagnosis was that some of the customers in Europe were leading users of cellphone testing software, and therefore were the first to adopt our diagnostic product, which was launched at the end of 2015. Already at the beginning of our series of discussions, we identified a problem in our launching of new products, which were released to the market before they were mature enough, and most of the complaints in Europe did indeed come in this context.

    Another thing that stood out in the difference between the continents: we have two hardware platforms. The first one includes all the software internally and it was very commonly used in North America. In Europe however, the market was divided between the platform that is prevalent in the US and a platform in which the hardware is a type of splitter/bridge, with the software being in the store's computer. We found out that in this product, the download time is significantly longer than for the first platform; this contributed to a lack of satisfaction in Europe compared to customers in North America.

The process of analyzing the information helped us crystallize towards the next steps, with the aim of improving products and customers support outside of North America.

Additional feedback we received related to our company's image – the company has lost its positioning as an innovator in recent years. I received this comment from the very beginning from our salespeople, who had heard it many times from customers.

The product plan for the next 18 months

This discussion lasted many hours, and its purpose was to define the products which we will decide to develop, with detailed work plans to be created over the course of the following two months.

Since it was clear to us that development of the products couldn't be carried out in addition to what is currently being developed, we made decisions in regard to products that we would stop developing and marketing.

As stated, decisions regarding the cancelation of products are always difficult and highly-charged. There will always be someone who will express the reasons for customer demand to retain an existing product, and explain how necessary it is. In this regard, we performed a detailed analysis before taking each decision to cancel one of our products.

What are we giving up?

1. As noted above, we decided at this point to put aside three products:

   - We decided to cancel one of three different hardware platforms, which didn't add any real value and could be replaced by any of the other two.

   - There was an old application product line, whose user interface quality and user experience was poor, and whose maintenance also consumed a lot of resources, so we decided to stop any investment in it.

     It is important to elaborate on this case. Our company had developed over the previous several years, an app to perform content transfer between phones, and also an app for troubleshooting. This platform didn't take off, and I will mention several reasons for this:

     ○ Each product was developed independently of other products, though much of the functionality was similar. This led to a situation in which each new function or feature had to be developed several times, each time to match the specific platform (H/W, SaaS, app, etc.): the products were characterized by different programming languages, different platforms, and different architectures. The maintenance of various products was too great a strain on the company, which lacked the resources, or a justification, given the current structure of the products, to bring them to the required level.

     ○ It was necessary to fundamentally change the user experience interface. There was feedback to this effect that was rightfully repeated. Such a change would require resources which weren't available, given the new products we wanted to develop. So, we decided to stop the developing of these products.

- Software as a Service (SaaS) Platform for Customer Service -

   It was decided that without a full understanding of the business model of potentials customers of such a product, we wouldn't continue to develop it, and because we didn't have the needed resources, in light of the things we decided to focus on, we would stop this product line.

As noted, we stopped or canceled nearly 50% of our company's products, However, that wasn't enough.

2. In the analysis that examined what development time was invested in, we found that 70% of our development time dealt with adapting products to specific customer requests. Our first decision was that for the coming year, we would limit the percentage of our development resources devoted to handling customer requests to 30%, and those that will be strictly limited to cosmetic changes (a drop from 70% to 30% within a period of several weeks!).

This decision, to reduce our development resources to support our customers' requests, a step that seemed trivial and turned out to a necessity, was difficult and complex, for two reasons:

- We had to inform our major customers that beyond certain changes, we wouldn't be making changes to the extent, and at the rate, they had become accustomed to in recent years. Some of them took this very hard, and threatened to cancel agreements, a response that I took into consideration, and which I was prepared to accept. Others, unfortunately a very small part of our customers, accepted the move with understanding, especially after we showed them how they would benefit from our move in less than a year – thanks to the new product that would enable them to do most of the modifications by themselves, independent of us.

The immediate result was that although orders weren't canceled, I had to personally visit ten of our larg customers in various parts of the world, and explain the move. It is important to note that despite all of our investment in facilitating the change, our move damaged relations with some of the customers, and they returned to a positive track only a year later, when they saw the new products.

♦ I was surprised to find out how difficult it was for the version release group (Delivery), those who were in contact with major customers, to convey the new message: There would be no more fundamental adjustments.

It must be understood that this group works in constant contact with those responsible at the customer for the product use level, and the delivery team had difficulty dealing with the pressure that the customers applied to them. Of course, senior management, who didn't always predict the intensity of the responses, was also responsible for this situation.

What should we develop in the next 18 months?

1. Since 90% of our company's revenues come from our hardware platform, which is what should provide us with the most revenue in the next 15 months at least, it was decided to strengthen this platform by adding a capability that would be considered a tie-breaker compared to all the other solutions available in the market.

   The ability to "clone" cellphone content of any kind, didn't exist, and we decided to develop it with both a short-term and long-term view. Think of a situation even if you have many gigabytes of content such as movies, pictures, apps, a cover photo, or any other content, after we have "cloned" the old phone to the new one in just a few minutes, in fact you couldn't distinguish between the old and new phone – everything would look exactly the same.

Developing such a capability, if designed correctly, could achieve the following objectives for us:

- Ensure income levels for the next budget year, since the ability in question could justify charging a higher price, compared to competing software solutions, to our present Tier1 customers – retail chains.
- We could actually charge a separate fee for this capability. The plan was to introduce the new capability as an application layer that ran on the hardware platform, with a dedicated annual license fee. This would increase the profit margin by 10%, since this involves software only.
- This development will be designed as a separate module, which we can implement "as is" on the SaaS platform that we will discuss below.
- This development fits in well with constructing our company's brand. We will expand on this issue when we talk about brand building.

2. At the same time, it was decided to develop a software-as-a-service (SaaS) version, which will comprise 95% of the functionality of our existing product and include smart settings that will enable every customer to make all the changes and definitions itself, all with the help of a configuration tool that will be an integral part of the product.

3. Similarly, it was decided to develop an application platform that will be part of the SaaS architecture platform, and will focus initially on transferring data between phones.

4. We decided to prepare the infrastructure for entry into the AMS market by developing a SaaS product for testing 40 phones simultaneously.

5. We decided to promote further entry into the AMS segment for the second-hand cellphones sales, by developing an application that will serve the Buyback vendors, by enabling them to perform an automatic process of diagnosing the phone condition and providing a suggested price, an ability that didn't exist in the market.

Summary of the off-site meeting

As you can imagine, discussions at the off-site meeting were long and complex, but in my opinion, we left the off-site meeting strengthened.

1. The AMS market has grown at a significantly faster pace than the retail market that we operate in. In addition, we also have technological components that fit this market, but we don't have enough products, expertise, and experience in the field.

    We decided to recruit a new product leader for the AMS market, so that we can enter this business, starting with the refurbishing and the Buyback companies.

2. We decided that our company would increase its activity in the retail market through a new retail chain SaaS platform, and an application platform for:

    ♦ Transferring data between phones (Content Transfer).

    ♦ Checking the phone's health (Diagnostics).

These products will expand our company's business operations outside the store, to the digital domain, that is, providing the same user experience regardless of the user's physical location, whether it is in the store, on the go, or at home. This expansion was supposed to double the potential revenue from the Tier1 market, and open up the Tier2 market, which is the same size.

Our long-term vision was that if we would become active in both the Retail and AMS markets, then 1 + 1 would add up to more than 2.

3. In order to expand our basket of products as described, we have reached the conclusion that there is a need to give up several products; it was decided to

   ♦ Cancel one of the three hardware platforms.
   ♦ Stop investing in an old application product line.
   ♦ Discontinue the development of SaaS platform Customer Service.

   The bottom line – we stopped development of, or eliminated, close to 50% of our company's products.

4. Reduce the time devoted to developing specific customer requirements from 70% to 30% of total development hours.

   The feeling at the end of the off-site meeting was excellent; we felt we managed to separate between developments which we invested a lot of energy in but don't generate much benefit, from identification of what is needed to get us onto a new path.

Forming a cohesive executive team

In the list of three goals of the two-day off-site meeting that was held on my first 100 days on the job, forming a cohesive executive team was defined as goal number one. But what defines a team as "cohesive?"

And an even more fundamental question: Why is forming a cohesive team important?

I faced the question of the common goal or the "common problem" many times when my job was to lead a change in a company. Is a decline in sales in 2019 just the problem of the sales leader or the marketing leader, or is it the problem of the whole organization, and all the members of the executive team? This example sharpens the issue of the executive management's functioning as a real team, working together to lead to significant changes.

I have decided to describe here some of the principles which in my opinion are essential in forming a cohesive executive team.

1. **Defining a vision and a shared goal that the management members identify with emotionally.**

The questions: "As a company, what is our vision? What is our goal?" sound trivial, but it's advisable to ask each member of the management team these questions, and see whether you get the same answers from all of them. Often, you will get different answers from the team members, or answers that relate to quantitative targets. Goals such as "sell 20% more..." or "get maximal profit for shareholders," do not generate emotional identification which results in team spirit, and thus the inner desire of team members to achieve the company's real goals declines.

Above all else, the management team should identify emotionally with the organization's vision and its purpose; otherwise, we'll get a make-believe team, and not a real team.

A real team or a make-believe team?

Katzenbach (1997) defines a real team as "two or more people with complementary skills that interact in a common cause which requires mutual cooperation between the members, and the functional contribution of each of them, while agreeing on goals, objectives, and work arrangement, with interdependence and mutual responsibility for the goals, and for the growth of the team members."

When comparing performance, a real team appears to be most effective in producing results.

In contrast, a make-believe team is defined as "two or more people with complementary skills who are required to operate within the framework of a team for a complex goal which requires teamwork, but do not agree about, or are not committed to the goals of the team." In such a team, the output is poor, and this situation even undermines the work of the individuals.

If we discover that the management team carries out all the "team rituals" (meetings, reports, setting common goals), but does not function in everyday life as a team, it is worthwhile to examine which of the components in the definition of a "real team" is missing, and accordingly to develop and promote teamwork, for example, by clarifying the shared vision, establishing trust among members, or creating mechanisms which will contribute to shared responsibility.

2. Knowing each other's goals

Understanding the objectives of other departments, and how the department manager chooses to achieve them, is essential for organizational coordination. For example, if the Marketing manager advocates transparency and dissemination of accurate data to its employees, but the Sales manager publicizes higher goals than those really planned in order to challenge their employees, the employees' conversations in the corridors will create confusion, speculation, and unnecessary tension. In addition, if each member of management is familiar with the work objectives and challenges of the other managers, a mutual contribution to the achievement of the goals will be possible.

We decided that we would first define the organization's overall goals for 2017, and from there every leader would summarize their own department's goals; then, the details of all the goals would be incorporated in a document that would be visible to all management members, and even beyond this – to the entire organization.

It is important to note, however, that I would not necessarily disclose every decision made to all employees. For example, if among the goals of a company were selling the company or closing a branch in a particular country, I wouldn't reveal such information to all employees.

We decided to complete the detailed definition of the goals, and to publicize them, by the end of the year (2016).

3. Defining roles and responsibilities

Because most processes are cross-departmental, we had to define in what way each department and its manager are involved in each of the company's processes.

Doing so led to a number of positive results:

- Everyone knew the boundaries of their responsibilities.
- Even if a manager is not fully responsible for a topic, they would nevertheless know the level of their involvement in that topic.
- In the course of defining responsibility and involvement in main processes, we created a detailed definition of each important process in our company.

We carried out the task of defining processes and management involvement by building an R&R (Roles & Responsibilities) table.

Here is an example of the result for several processes:

Phase	Activity	Function										
		Sales Engineer	Sales Manager	Sales Ops & Logistics	Customer Support	Product Management	Quality (Processes)	R&D (QA, SW Dev, System Eng, Research)	Project Manager	Product Marketing	Customer Success	Finance / Legal	Security officer/ IT
Pre-Sale	RFx/Deal Review	R	A	C	R	R	R	R	R	C		R	R
	Off the Shelf Pilot	A	C	R	R	I	R	I	A	I			
	Pilot change Request	R	C			R	R	R	A				C
	Contracts & Legal	R	A	R	R	R	R		R	R		R	C
	Quote	C	A	R		I	R					R	

Definition of responsibility level:

R	Responsible	Assigned to do the task
A	Accountable	Final decision maker, owner of the task
C	Consultant	Must be consultant before decisions are made
I	Informed	Must be informed

Building an R&R table takes time, and demands the intense concentration of all management members. It took us more than six months to complete this task.

4. Conflict management

Conflicts occur all the time. Most conflicts are built into the workings of the organization.

Here are examples of conflicts that come up in most organizations:

- A problem with a product for an important customer pops up, but if the development team diverts resources to solve it, a new product will not be released in time, after the company had already committed itself to a specific launch date.

- A salesperson is negotiating a large deal, on the condition that a certain capability is developed, but in order to include it in the product, the next development version must be modified. This means, among other things, that the upcoming version will not include a different capability that was already committed, that may foil a deal another salesperson on another continent made, if not delivered.

There may, of course, be personal conflicts between managers.

The CEO's role, in my view, is to encourage direct dialogue between staff members, and to promote visible and observable management resolution of conflicts. Hidden conflict resolution, performed within the CEO's office alone, without the entire executive team's active participation, establishes the CEO's as a "problem solver"; this reduces the importance of the other members of the management team, and creates a hidden layer of usually baseless speculation and suspicion that damages the trust among the team members. It is very important that conflicts be solved by the senior management members themselves, without the CEO, and that the conflict's existence, the alternatives, and the agreed-upon solution, be fully visible to the entire management team, not just to the CEO.

5. **Mutual responsibility**

Since each manager is usually an expert in the field they are responsible for (marketing, finance, sales, information systems, etc.), producing a manager's responsibility for someone else's territory is not a simple process.

In addition to updating and reporting at executive management meetings, it is worthwhile to develop processes in which senior managers are responsible for cross-organizational tasks, and thus become partners in what goes on in other departments. For example: if the annual work plan includes a task such as "developing team spirit and promoting employee retention" or "streamlining and improving profitability," the appointment of a senior management team member as a leader of the task will require them to be involved in other departments activity, harnessing other senior managers to the task, and reporting on the task's progress at the different levels.

In general, what is the added value of all members of management as a group?

The synergy in the management's work is expressed in the sum of the functional contribution of each of its members. The potential contribution of each member of the team is composed of their expertise and knowledge in the field for which they are responsible, and their personal skills and talents. For example, an analytical person can contribute to the team in everything related to the attention to details, proposing of alternatives, and completing tasks, while a creative person can help solve complex problems, or to innovate and inject energy into the organization.

6. Breaking up "coalitions"

Within the overall senior management team, sometimes unofficial sub-teams (coalitions) are created on the basis of seniority in the organization, interpersonal chemistry or complementary content areas. The danger in the existence of an unofficial sub-team, especially if it is perceived as close to the CEO, is that the other members of senior management do not feel like full partners in the executive management, so they don't contribute their full potential to team synergy. When from time to time a small team from within the executive team is required to make decisions or to lead a topic, it is recommended that the CEO diversify the mix of managers selected for these small teams, and not create a permanent "sub-cabinet."

7. **Recognition and public appreciation of the executive team's work**

The work of the members of the management team, their commitment, and their loyalty to the CEO and to the common purpose, are generally only recognized as a result of a crisis. But it's recommended that the senior management's teamwork be treated as a permanent component in corporate improvement analysis, and to appreciate and praise cooperation among managers on an ongoing basis, which will encourage similar behavior ongoing, and contribute to team spirit.

Building middle management and growth infrastructure

When you prepare a company for growth, one of your challenges is building a proper infrastructure which will enable growth. This requires work on two levels:

1. In terms of human infrastructure – building a corporate middle management level: the middle management level is a key factor in the ability of organizations to formulate and implement a coordinated and relevant strategy.

2. An infrastructure for growth should include both a structural and a functional infrastructure. In both cases, this is an infrastructure that will produce similar results both when the organization is small (in the number of employees, income, customers) and when it grows.

An organization with 40 employees and 20 customers has requirements similar to those of an organization with 300 employees and 200 customers. Examples I will address further on include:

- R&D structure.
- Building a data base infrastructure.
- Building an infrastructure for Customer Success.
- Customer support and more.

In this chapter, we will focus on our process of building the middle-management level during the months following our off-site meeting, and then we will discuss building the necessary infrastructure to improve efficiency, profitability, and growth.

Middle management is a function that connects two levels – the senior managerial level, which usually deals with more strategic issues or problems which require a concentration of lateral effort, and the operational level, which deals with the daily routine of the company's activity.

One can say that the middle management level is between two organizational levels which are conducted with completely different logics. On the part of senior management, an attempt is made to promote organizational processes, while from below there is an attempt to cope with very specific day-to-day challenges, which are related to daily work, and which arise from the field.

If you go down to a more detailed level, you can note that the middle managers have two key roles:

1. Transformation of business plans into practical work plans and their realization.
2. Managing the environment in which the work is actually performed. The middle manager's job is both to make sure that the work is done, and also to support employees' emotional ties to the workplace, to the company as a whole, and to other employees in the organization. In fact, the middle managers are the ones who determine the state of mind of the employees.

In well-run companies, information flows in both directions of the management chain – both up and down. Middle level managers receive guidelines from the organization's leadership, and convert them into action plans for teams and employees. They must explain why each directive is important, and what the role of each and every employee is in implementing company strategy. In addition, they receive information from employees who are at the forefront of the company's activity, and transfer it up the management chain.

If the middle management is not performing well, those who suffer are both the managers above them, and the employees subordinate to them.

In general, it is not easy to be a middle manager, especially one who has not received the required support and training.

When they do not receive the support they need from the organization in order to grow and cope with job challenges, middle level managers may feel stuck and frustrated. When this happens to a middle level manager, their motivation is impaired and this will leak, to some degree, down to their subordinates. This will harm how much the employees care about the organization, and will prevent them from fully understanding why their work is important, and how it relates to the vision and goals of the organization. A strong middle management level is a necessary infrastructure for organizational growth when things are going well, and even more so in times of crisis, when the organization wishes to cut back and streamline, while at the same time maintaining its goals.

So what steps did we, as the senior management, take to promote the middle management level in the organization?

1. The first step was to define who is a middle manager. Is it just those who manage subordinates, or are domain managers who lead areas of activity but do not manage subordinates also included?

    We decided to include both categories of managers.

2. We defined the structure of the meetings of middle level managers, the meetings' contents, and the time intervals between them.

- It was decided to convene the Middle management forum once every quarter, and also whenever there is news with a high value to the company, or when organizational changes are about to take place.

   The quarterly meetings will present to middle management the main materials that will be presented to the Board of Directors, mainly matters relating to the company's business activity, and how it matches the company's strategy and goals, as the company's performance, for better or for worse. Particularly sensitive topics will not be presented.

- Middle management meetings were attended by senior management. As CEO, I made a presentation at these meetings, and encouraged questions.

   In practice, the forum also helped us channel two-way communication with the employees, and also contributed to the creation of a good relationship between the participants, which in itself contributed to reducing the tensions between the departments, and to improving communication between them.

Building an infrastructure for growth

As noted at the beginning of the chapter, infrastructure for growth should include both structural infrastructure and functional infrastructure.

Structural infrastructure usually refers to those bodies that are always in a state of resizing, or those whose number of tasks is constantly changing.

A few examples:

1. R&D department.
2. Professional services.

3. The production team – which must deal with changing production quantities (as a result of seasonal production or any other reason that repeats itself and causes great variance at different periods), and/or with a change in the number of product lines.
4. Technical support or customer support.
5. Customer Service.

In some cases, under certain conditions, the company can compensate for the continues resizing need by means of processes that attempt to cope with rapid changes, but we will not address this possibility in this book.

Here we will refer to a number of infrastructures that we changed in this specific case in order to adapt the organization to the strategy defined by management.

Adapting the R&D department's structure to growth

A significant structural change that we made relates to the R&D department, which we will describe in detail in the section "Changing the structure of R&D."

Customer Success

There are three main questions in the context of this function:

1. **Purpose?** Customer retention.
2. **What is the essence of the Customer Success function?** As its name indicates, ensuring successful use of the product by the customer.
3. **How do you measure the performance success level of this function?** Percentage of license renewal.

How do we connect the customer's successful use of the product and license renewal? To answer this question, I will describe the basic assumptions that guided the management's thinking on this subject.

- There is a strong connection between the level of use and the percentage of renewal of licenses: the more the customer uses the product, the more their business activity will be dependent on it, which will be translated into renewal of the license.

- Therefore, it is the Customer Success function's responsibility to closely follow the level of usage and its quality (which functionality is used more, and which less), so that defects or problems with the product can be detected. The information collected can be passed to product management with recommendations for changes, or to the QA group in the case of bugs.

However, our basic assumption (that was found correct, and I will provide examples below), was that there are other variables, that are independent of us, that affect product usability. That is, even if the product is functioning perfectly, there are other factors that define the level of use.

The Customer Success function's role is to understand these variables, and to formulate ways to help the customer deal with them.

By the very fact that we understand all external variables that have a direct impact on the level of product usability, we become sort of experts, or, if you will, can serve as consultants to our customers on issues that are not necessarily directly related to our product, but directly affect it. I'll give some examples, some of which I referred to in previous chapters:

- ♦ The level of use of our diagnostic product was low.

What is this product? If a customer enters the store and complains of a problem with the phone, within a few minutes we could diagnose the problem, and in most cases, we could correct it, including when the problem is a virus, or conflicting applications drivers.

After extensive investigation, we found that, in many cases, the low use of this product wasn't related to the product itself, but how the store conducts its business. While the store employees receive a commission for selling, they don't do so for helping the customer to solve a problem with the phone. Because of this, the store employees skips over such customers, and tries to focus exclusively on selling phones. In practice, they send a phone with a problem straight to the repair center, rather than trying to solve the problem on the spot.

How did we deal with this situation?

We built a simple business model, which described to the retail chains' senior management the amount of money they would be able to save, and how much they could improve their profitability, if they used our product in the store, and avoided sending the phone to the repair center.

Within less than a year, we saw an improvement in processes in some of the retail chains – the chains prevented a phone from being sent to a repair center if it hadn't been tested first with our device in the store.

- ◆ In one of the retail chain stores, we found a significant drop in the level of use of our diagnostic product. After investigation, it became clear that the store manager limited the time that could be devoted to dealing with phone problems to a given number of minutes per customer, and since it wasn't possible to comply with this limitation while using our application, this resulted in a considerable reduction in the use of our product. Again, this was a case of a process that was seemingly unrelated to us, but directly affects the use of the product.

As a result of this case, and with the understanding that dealing with the problematic phones should take as little time as possible, we changed the application's data flow, so that within half of the total time, the user sees initial results, while at the same time the product continued deeper analysis. This process change helped us with that customer, and in general, contributed to the improvement of the product.

With the projected growth in sales of our Software as a Service (SaaS) solutions, whose customer payment method in this case is through an annual license, the license renewal percentage and its price was set as the heart of the strategy to increase the company's revenues.

Therefore, we decided to adopt a platform that identifies a low level of usability, warns the customer and the account manager about this, and helps the customer to improve it.

What were the main requirements for this infrastructure platform?

- Monitoring of usage level (number of transactions performed during a given period of time) real-time.

- Tracking the quality of use (which function is used more, and which less).

- Notifying both the customer and the account manager if the level of use is lower than nominal values (which can be set in several ways), and a recommendation to the customer how to improve their use of our product, and an increase in our customer follow-up.

- Notifying the QA manager and product manager if any process which is part of the software did not end successfully, to enable detection of defects in use, or problems with the product. The information gathered is automatically delivered to the Product Manager and the QA Group Manager.

- Enabling the Product Manager to set up a dashboard by customer group (similar characteristics), including diving for details, and alerts in real time.
- Enabling the product manager to define a "customer score" based on various parameters. The goal of this score is to identify a change in the customer's use level over time, and also to compare the customer's score to that of other customers which are part of the same group.

The result of our overall investment in infrastructure and in personnel was an increase in the license renewal percentage.

How do we calculate license renewal percentage? What is the correct goal?

Although it may seem obvious how the renewal percentage should be calculated, there are some alternate possibilities that should be considered:

1. Renewal percentage by the number of customers.
2. Renewal percentage by the number of licenses; this may be different from renewal by number of customers (because one customer may have multiple licenses).
3. Renewal percentage by revenue, which also can be represented by different indices, such as MRR (Monthly Recurring Revenue) or ARR (Annual Recurring Revenue).

We've presented three options here (there are more). When should we use each of them?

- Let's start with renewal by number of customers: Suppose we have 100 customers who need to renew the license this year, only 90 renewed, meaning 90% renewal; that's simple. Let's spend a minute explaining the benefit of measuring renewal by customers and what are the limitations. Customers are the most important for anyone who sells a product or services. Without customers, we do not have the right to exist as a business and therefore we must measure our ability to retain our customers, hence, customer renewal rate is the first parameter we will look into. Even though calculating this parameter in my opinion is mandatory, it is not always enough.

  It is only sufficient in a situation where we have one type of license, and each customer holds one license; in that case, calculating renewals based on number of customers is actually the same as renewal by number of licenses. So if we return to the previous example where we have 100 customers all having the same license and each customer holds a single license, then we have 100 customers and 100 licenses, and then if 90 licenses are renewed, then we have 90% renewal of licenses and this is the same as renewal rate for customers.

  According to another example, we have 100 customers but this time 90 customers each have a license of $100 and 10 customers each have a license whose annual cost is $1,000. Therefore, the total annual income equals 90 multiplied by $100 + 10 multiplied by $1,000, so we have an annual income of $19,000. Just to take the example one step forward, let's assume that all 10 customers with an annual license of $1,000 each, did not renew their license, so still out of the 100 customers, 90 renewed so 90% of the customers renewed, but in terms of revenue we are seeing a 53% drop from $19,000 to $9,000 which is a very significant drop which was not reflected when looking at the 90% customer's renewal rate we just saw.

- Another option is calculating renewal by number of licenses. When should we use this index? When the customer can have a number of licenses.

    Returning to the previous example: 90 customers have a license of $100 and 10 customers' annual license cost is $1,000. Then, in this case too, if the 10 customers each with a $1,000 annual license did not renew, then the percentage renewal of the customers or of the licenses is the same - 90%. So in the situation where each customer has one license, the percentage of renewals according to customers and licenses is identical and not sufficient, as we don't see the 53% drop in revenue.

    Measuring the percentage of renewal by licenses is only effective if all customers have a similar license. For example, let's say that all 100 of our customers have licenses of one kind of $100 per year, but this time we assume they hold a different number of licenses - 90 customers each hold a single license at an annual cost of $100 and 10 other customers each have 10 licenses of $100 per year. In other words, the 90 customers hold 90 licenses of $100 and 10 customers hold 100 licenses together, and we have all together 190 licenses each for $100. If all those 10 customers who hold 10 licenses did not renew, the result this time is that 90% of the **customers** have renewed, but only 90 out of the 190 **licenses** were renewed: this is a loss of 53% of the licenses and it helps us to identify that there is a problem.

- Here we need another parameter and it is the third we will discuss: renewal based on revenue.

    Renewal based on Revenue can be represented by various parameters such as MRR or ARR.

MRR - Monthly Recurring Revenue. This refers to the monthly turnover of the Company from its subscriber customers, mainly in reference to software products using subscription model.

ARR - Annual Recurring Revenue. And again, the annual turnover of the company from its subscriber customers.

In the case of our example, the ARR at the beginning is $19,000 and at the end of the year its only $9,000, here you see the revenue drop of 53%.

Some more examples:

Example 1a:

Customer A has an annual subscription of $ 10,000.

Customer B has an annual subscription of $ 100,000.

Customer A canceled, and customer B renewed.

According to the number of licenses, the renewal rate is 50%. According to revenue from the license renewals, the renewal rate is 91%.

Example 1b: Now we will change Example 1a slightly: Customer A canceled their license, and customer B renewed their license after a price rise of 10%. By number of licenses, the renewal percentage is still 50%. By revenue, the renewal percentage is now 100%.

The more different your contracts and customers are, the more important it is to understand the characteristics of license renewal according to different factors.

Thoroughly understanding the licenses renewal percentage characteristics is critical to streamlining SaaS-based business operations.

It is important to emphasize that since you are the ones

who define how the renewal percentage is calculated, you will probably choose more than one way.

I do want to raise a number of additional issues as material for thought, and in order to raise awareness of subjects that you are likely to encounter:

1. Our customers were stores. How do we relate to stores that closed for some reason? Of course, their owners did not renew their licenses, but their failure to renew their license was not because they were dissatisfied with our product.

2. How do we relate to a customer who renewed a license not as soon as it expired, but rather only a certain period of time (a week/a month) later?

3. How do we relate to a chain of stores that decided on one bright day to leave the mobile phone market entirely? This chain will not renew its license for our products, but not because of dissatisfaction with our products; it simply pulled out of the market.

What is the right target to set for the renewal percentage?

There are two types of targets to consider. The first should be maintaining, or constantly improving, year after year, the company's license renewal percentage.

The second type refers to the license renewal percentage in your industry; in that case, it's important to set a target of X% higher than the accepted industry rate.

In the context of the Customer Success function, it is important to note that I have seen this position defined differently in different organizations, and similarly, the targets and the definition of success are different.

Building an online license purchase and renewal infrastructure

As already mentioned, we set a goal to come out with a Software as a Service (SaaS) platform which would enable us to increase our target market in the following areas:

1. Expanding business operations with existing Tier1 customers (mainly cellular operators) from solutions designed for use only in the store, to ones that can be used outside the store (on the move and at home) as well, for the growing market sector of online purchasers.

2. Significant increase in business activity with Tier2 customers, a market sector in which we were almost inactive. The reason was, as noted in the previous chapters, that their business model leaves a small profit margin in comparison to our Tier1 customers. The Software as a Service (SaaS) solution, which is significantly lower cost than the hardware platform, will allow us to serve this market sector.

3. The market sector that we did not serve at all, and is considered large, includes:

    - Tier3 customers – single stores and chains of less than 50 branches.
    - The entire prepaid world, which includes a significant portion of Asian countries, South America, and 20% of the European market.

In the prepaid world, store owners cannot predict how many customers will come in to receive our service, so they prefer to pay according to the number of transactions, and not to purchase fixed monthly or annual packages (of course, there will always be exceptions).

When dealing with Tier3's market segment, in which purchases are per each individual store or a small group of stores, we cannot achieve positive Return On Investment (ROI), unless everything is done completely automatically, through our website.

The same is true for the purchase of a transaction or a transaction package by one store or a group of stores. In all these cases, the only way to make the sale and earn a profit is to eliminate any human intervention in the sales process. And this was the essence of the project to build an automatic, online infrastructure for the sale of licenses and transactions, and renewal of licenses – an e-commerce infrastructure.

It is important to understand the complexity of selling transactions. There are two cases which should be addressed:

1. The simple case is that a store purchases for example a package of 100 transactions.

   The following variables should be considered here:

   ♦ The subject of time; since we as vendors want to record income and not to provide our service for an indefinite period of time, we would like to limit the transaction package's validity period. For how long is a package usually valid? The time periods mostly range from one month to one year.

   ♦ The system knows whether the transaction process was successful. Do we count the transaction whether it ended successfully or not? While it's clear that a successful transaction is counted, what about an unsuccessful one? There are actually two main scenarios:

   (a) the system failed and did not complete the transaction due to a malfunction.

   (b) the transaction did not end because the customer decided to stop it.

   I will leave it to the reader to decide on the solutions.

2. The more complex case is a situation where the company has several services, all of which are aimed at the same market, and are purchased as different licenses or as various transaction packages.

That is, the store that in the previous case purchased a package of 100 transactions, is interested in three services, and therefore will be required to purchase three different packages of 100 transactions, when in fact it has the same limited number of customers, which will undoubtedly make it difficult to buy so many packages.

The situation is even more complicated when it comes to a large, world-wide prepaid chain which wants to provide all the services, but it cannot predict the level of use of each service.

We also intended to provide three different services, and deliberated how to simplify dealing with stores and chains. What made things complicated was that one of the services was very unique, and we evaluated its value as higher than that of the other two.

In the end, as part of the effort to simplify working with the smaller chains, we decided to sell all three services at the same price, which allows the same store to still purchase a package of 100 transactions which supported all the services.

Online customer support

Customer support is a major challenge in any company. This challenge increases as the number of customers grows, and their geographic dispersion and their multiplicity of languages grow as well. Our company already faced this challenge, and it was expected that within a year, when all of our new activities would come to fruition, the complexity of customer support would be even greater. Therefore, we decided to build a customer support infrastructure, in parallel to the existing current one which is detailed in other chapters.

The cost of customer support is a significant component of the product cost. Therefore, in order to improve gross profit, it is important, on the one hand, to maintain a good level of customer support, and on the other hand, to adopt approaches aimed at reducing its cost.

The direction many companies turn to is building avenues of support not by way of the company's employees. Here are some examples:

1. Establishment of forums that indeed are controlled by a company support person, but whose goal is that customers themselves answer other customers' questions, which reduces the need to increase support personnel.

2. A relatively new field is the chatbot. A chatbot is a type of software product that specializes in managing textual conversations with people, designed to be as natural as possible. The conversation's purpose can be marketing, customer service consulting, or training. There are two main types of chatbots, which differ in the complexity of the software that simulates conversation:

    ♦ A chatbot with a prescribed set of rules or behaviors. The sophistication of this chatbot is limited, and it has already been in the market for many years.

    ♦ The new generation of chatbots, which uses artificial intelligence to 'understand' language. In this case, the chatbot 'understands' many formulations, and improves itself over time in its responses to the wording of its questioners.

3. Presenting a short video repository that answers frequently asked questions, or deals with the most common faults. Short

videos that can provide an answer within a few dozen seconds will encourage customers to watch them instead of turning to human support.

There are good tools to test the videos' quality, and to determine if they do actually provide the necessary answers, which helps to improve them.

4. A list of pre-made Q&A that can be reached by searching. This is a method that has existed for many years, and what is important here is to choose the best search engines in order to display the most relevant answers.

It is customary to combine the different channels, and, at the end of providing answers in one channel, to lead the customer to another channel. This method also gives another indication of the quality of each channel separately, and with time, and with the help of a type of AB Testing, will make it possible to decide which channel to direct to which type of customer, depending on the question or problem presented.

When adopting a complementary approach as described here, it is important to define the goals.

Examples of measuring variables that reflect the effectiveness of online customer support:

1. The number of requests for human response (as a percentage of end customers and as a percentage of total inquiries) every month.

2. The level of customer satisfaction with the service – it is very important to maintain the same method for calculating the satisfaction level over the years, to make a representative comparison possible.

3. The number of customers who used each of the channels each month – here we usually measure the trend.

4. The level of repeated customer use of the specified channels.

We decided to adopt the use of all the aforementioned methods, but we were not yet ready to set targets for all the above four variables.

Perpetual or subscription license

Over the course of several months, the executive team began to understand that there is a built-in problem with the type of license we sell – a perpetual license.

As we delved into the issue of license renewals, we realized that this model, in our case, contributes to a low percentage of maintenance renewals, and, on the other hand, creates frustrated customers. In other words, everyone loses.

What is the difference between the license types?

The perpetual license model was the dominant method for selling most software licenses over the last 30 years.

A perpetual software license allows the customer to use the software indefinitely.

Along with a perpetual software license, the vendor usually provides, during the initial period (typically 1 year), technical support and software updates. After this initial period, the vendor will offer a software upgrade or a support package that includes continued updates and technical support; the cost of the annual support package is usually around 20% of the cost of the software.

The alternative to a perpetual license is a subscription license. This model grants the right to use the software for a certain period of time. After this period, the license must be renewed if the customer wishes to continue using the software. You can look at the subscription licensing model as a type of service; it is referred to as SaaS, Software-as-a-Service, and as with any service, it is given for a predefined period of time and after that you need to continue to pay for it just like with other type of service, such as a cellular service, cable TV etc. In the subscription license model, the license already includes software updates, and some level of technical support.

For several years, surveys have been conducted to examine the level of use of the various models. An annual survey asked a variety of software vendors in different markets what licensing model generates most of their revenue, and how they expect the licensing mix to change. While there indeed is a variance between the different markets, the general answer is quite similar. For 2017, approximately 66% of the vendors' revenues derived from perpetual licenses, and 34% of the revenue came from subscription licenses.

It is also apparent that in recent years there has been a noticeable trend in the software world to switch from a perpetual to a subscription license and Software as a Service (SaaS).

This change is happening simultaneously with the software manufacturers moving the software infrastructure from a local installation (on premises) to the cloud.

You can find many examples: Microsoft 365, Google Cloud, and Salesforce, all offer an option for a subscription license.

With regard to small and medium-sized companies, it seems that investors are ready to absorb temporary reduction of revenues and cash flow with subscription licenses in order to generate an ongoing flow of income (recurring revenue), and this is reflected in the generous revenue multipliers investors use in estimating the value of companies operating subscription license model (SaaS); companies that offer subscription licenses are attractive to investors.

Let's examine the subject in more depth:

Which model is better?

It is important to review several variables and understand how each one affects the vendor and customer. We will mention the most important ones:

1. Revenue recognition – the income from a perpetual license will be recognized at the time of the delivery of the software, or when installation is complete. In the model of subscription licensing, revenue recognition occurs only with use, i.e., each and every month.

2. Cash flow – this factor similar to revenue recognition. Payment for a perpetual license is made, in whole or in part, after delivery of the software, when the installation is complete. In case of subscription licensing, the payment will be each month (or quarter or year) in advance. The difference is substantial. For example, for a perpetual licensed software whose cost is $100,000, the equivalent payment when you convert it to a subscription licensing price is, say, $3,000 a month or $36,000 a year, a very significant difference in cash flow and revenue recognition.

3. Where the software is installed – if the product is installed locally by the customer or on a dedicated cloud, in most cases the license will be perpetual. Where the software is on the cloud in a multi-tenant configuration, the license will be a subscription type. That is, as we will enable our customers to take advantage of virtualization and the cloud, subscription license will become the norm.

4. Type of customer - for small businesses or private customers, it is reasonable to assume that a monthly payment of $10 will be preferable to a one-time payment of $300 or $400. In addition, there are other benefits of a subscription license from the customer's point of view – the updates are continuous, and, of course, the customer can discontinue using the software at any time.

   In this case, the vendor should calculate the cost of 'acquisition'; that is, how much it costs the vendor to get a customer to buy a license (marketing: advertising, buying leads, etc.). If, for example, the cost of a customer acquisition is $40, the company will recover its investment in this purchase only after four months, and it must be taken into account that a customer can cancel the use of the product after a shorter time. Choosing the license model in this case takes a lot of thought, and the company must respond in accordance with the renewal data that accumulates, but we will not go deeper than this in this book.

5. Customer accounting practice – especially for large customers, and when it comes to expensive software, we must find out whether customers prefer capital expenditure, in which case the customer will be inclined towards a perpetual license, or operational expenditure, in which case it will prefer a subscription license.

6. Additional issues that the organization should consider include:

   - How do we calculate commissions for sales/marketing personnel? In the perpetual license model, a salesperson is normally rewarded immediately, after the closing the deal, or after receipt of the payment. In the subscription licensing model, where there is a risk of the customer canceling the subscription, more complex compensation models need to be created.

   - If you use regional distributors, what is the commission structure for subscription license sales?

What is the risk of switching from a perpetual to a subscription license?

One of the largest "headaches" for a company that decides to switch from a perpetual to subscription licensing is the impact on revenue and cash flow that occurs when, suddenly, the large disposable revenue that the company is accustomed to recognizing from the perpetual license disappears, and is replaced by periodic payments. To avoid this shock, the organization must prepare laterally:

1. The Finance Department must produce alternatives to cash flow. Here are a number of examples:

    - These days, loans can be obtained at convenient terms, calculated according to a certain multiple on the Monthly Recurring Revenue (MRR).
    - For many types of software, especially those targeting businesses, customers can be requested to subscribe to a minimum period of a year (or more) and pay the annual fee in advance.
    - The company can decide that, for a given period of time, it will allow certain customers to continue to purchase a perpetual license, so that the transition can be made gradually.

2. Marketing and sales departments:

    - Special promotion and an attempt to increase the rate of sales, due to the transition to subscription licensing.
    - Dealing with the entire issue of commissions to sales managers and marketing channels.

An example of switching between license types

Consider the following example:

- The company adds 12 new customers each year (one new customer each month).

- Each customer pays $100,000 for a perpetual license. After a year, such a customer pays $18,000 every year for maintenance (support and software updates).

- After 24 months, i.e. at the beginning of the third year, all new customers purchase subscription model and pay $35,000 a year.

- The veteran customers will continue to pay $18,000 each year for support and software updates.

Outcome:

- As you can see from the following diagram, at the transition point, after 24 months, there is a decrease of 40% in cash flow.

- Only in the third year of the transition between models, will the company recover, and even increase, its revenue and cash flow.

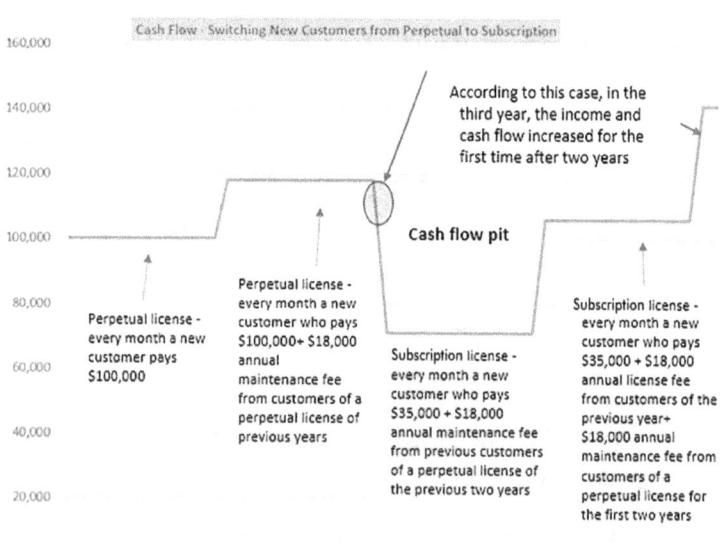

Back to the case of our company – the licenses that our company sold were perpetual licenses, and after the initial period, which was one or three years, the company offered an annual support package that included software updates, bug fixes, and most importantly – up-to-date support for new phones.

A basic and fundamental problem we had as a result of selling perpetual licenses was created when customers delayed in purchasing a support and update package. This package, as mentioned, also included support of new phones, and therefore if the support package was not purchased, utilization and level of use of our products declined, because as time passed, the product supported fewer and fewer phones (since new phones which were released since the package expired were not supported). This further severely affected the percentage of maintenance license renewals. There was another important parameter: when we sold a hardware/software platform for three years, in most cases it was part of a leasing program. From an accounting point of view, the sale of a perpetual software with hardware, when all the package is sold in leasing, allows recognition of most of the revenue already in the first year, also including the hardware. That is, the budget pit which will be created with a transition to a subscription license will be even greater than that of a switch between solutions that include software only. Thus, starting from the next fiscal year, in which a high percentage of sales will be based on software platforms without hardware, by selling subscription licenses, we will have a budgetary hole for the first few years, and we will have to deal with it, mainly through increased sales on the one hand, and on the other hand, the increase in profitability should help us bridge some of the gap.

Changing the Research & Development structure

This chapter was written by Moshe Lipsker, who served as R&D vice president throughout the period I was CEO.

(The chapter includes many technical concepts. We tried to add an explanation right next to most of them).

In this document, I will try to describe the process of my assuming the position of vice president for R&D, the vision and strategic plan that the company's executive management decided to implement on the basis of some of their findings, and the technological revolution that was required in order to carry out the strategic plan and its tactical derivatives. Part of this revolution was reflected in a large organizational change that eventually transformed the organization into a goal-directed agile organization capable of extremely high performance.

Assuming office

Upon starting my position, I examined the organization from four different angles:

1. Business.

2. Products.

3. Technology.
4. People (+ organizational functions) and processes.

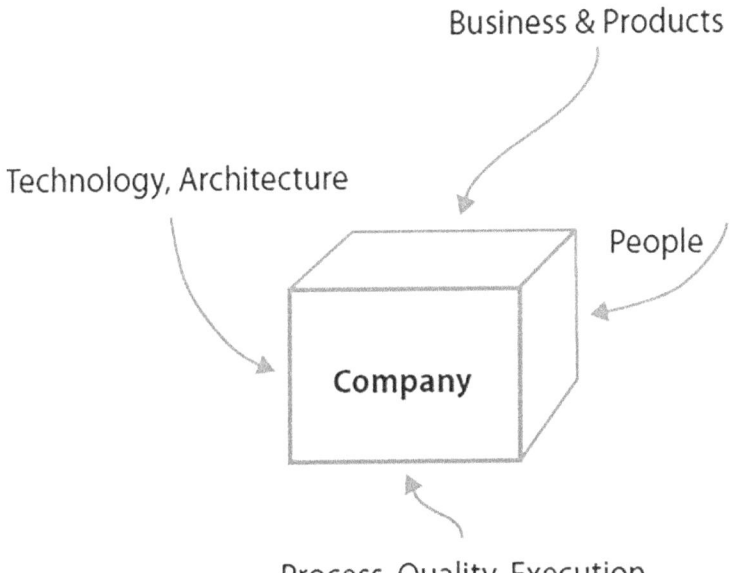

Business aspect – main findings

- Our company sold mainly hardware, and profit margins were low.
- The main customers who allowed themselves to buy expensive hardware were Tier1 cellular operators' retail chains – very large customers – which resulted in a few large transactions, without giving us any real ability to expand our business operations to many additional medium-sized and small customers, and thus we didn't have access to most of the market.
- These large customers had many demands, which made the R&D group tailor unique solutions to certain customers,

instead of building off-the-shelf products. Return on investment (ROI) of this method was very low, and it was clear that the R&D focus wasn't in the right place.

- Our main revenue was based on data transferring services. The diagnostics service consumed a lot of the R&D resources, but there was no match between the R&D investment in the field of diagnostics and the revenue it generated.
- The organization was oriented towards a short-term sales view, rather than towards vision and long-term strategy.

Products – main findings

- We had many products, with many unsuccessful attempts (a lot of the products delivered to customers were only at the elementary Proof of Concept level), without a clear focus on what would have the desired effect on our business.
- The quality of our products isn't high enough, i.e. we have products that work only partially for customers in the field. Products were released just at the feasibility test level, without an orderly development process, i.e.:
  - Clear definition of version contents.
  - A clear plan for implementation of the defined content.
  - A progressive and regressive testing plan for the developed content.
  - Alpha and beta testing plans.
  - A process of releasing zero-fault products.
- Obsolete User Interface (UI) and User Experience (UX). The products were mostly technology-oriented (towards technical people), and less oriented towards simplicity of use by the users.

- Low use of our diagnostic products, and low percentage of runs ending successfully.

Technology – main findings

- Old technology (over 10 years old).
- We use a very cumbersome and heavy C ++ programming language infrastructure layer that required rewriting the communication with the phone devices and the protocols for each type of cellphone in the market, rather than using up-to-date libraries that would allow generic connection for any advanced device, without having to rewrite protocols or connectivity for each one.
- The old code didn't allow a desirable development rate – it was characterized by slow feature velocity and slow delivery cadence.

The infrastructure layer described above included two million lines of code, while the application layer developed in .NET contained a million lines of code. In addition to the uncontrollable amount of code, there was a great deal of unnecessary complexity in the architecture, and as a derivative, also in the code.

The complicated architecture was inefficient, which led to very slow development, since any small modification required full regression testing and very long development processes.

- The way we transferred data was designed for older generation cellphones (feature phones) and not the newer smartphones.
- The diagnostic service had limited technological depth.

People (+ organizational functions) and processes – main findings

- There is too much "flag waving" of customer problems by salespeople and project managers. We dealt with too many problems from the field as a result of quality issues. Any problem with a customer didn't pass through any filter, but rather came straight to R&D; this situation didn't allow for orderly, focused work on future development.

- Lack of control – we suffer from a lack of clear organizational processes, leading to an absence of orderly development processes, as detailed in Figure 1.

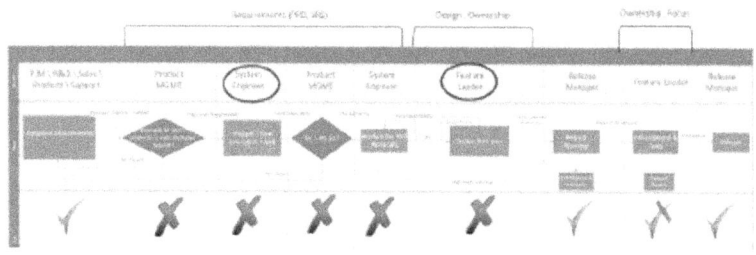

Figure 1 – Typical development process
(X indicates something missing in our development process)

- There is a lack of internal communication:

    Sales ↔ Product management,

    Product management ↔ R&D,

    R&D ↔ QA,

    R&D and QA ↔ Customer support.

- There is no clear definition of roles and responsibility (R&R) among all organizational functions.

- The lack of clear definitions for R&D (there is a lack of a system engineering function) caused incorrect understanding of the users' demands, which resulted in inaccurate development.

- The responsibility for releasing the product from R&D was that of the single Release Manager, creating a bottleneck which inevitably forced a slow development pace and many delays in releasing versions (at the rate of a version every four months).

Vision and strategic plan

As a result of the above findings, the organization's management decided on the following vision:

Switching from hardware to SaaS software, which will enable access to services which will lead to an increase in the use of our products (by a factor of three), and as a result a large database will be created which will constitute the Artificial Intelligence (AI) infrastructure for a variety of predictive capabilities on smartphones.

The three-year strategy as shown in Figure 2:

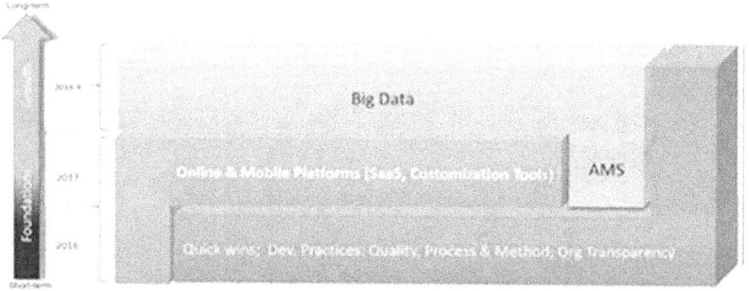

Figure 2 – Three-year strategy

Stage one – building the foundation

- Organizational transparency by way of a Business Intelligence (BI) tool.

For example, a service level agreement (SLA) with customers in the case of a request for development or complaints from the field, and support for visual tools.

- Improving code quality - deepening technology of basic services, and writing several patents.

- Ordering organizational processes and developmental processes – establishing organizational functions such as system engineering and architecture and development leaders (Feature leaders), to support developmental processes and create a clear source of responsibility throughout the development phase.
- Development + QA - Combining testing and development into one integrated group, and a closer connection of the product management group to the integrated development group.
- Switching to "sprints" (development cycles) of two weeks, and releasing a server-side version every two weeks, and a client-side version every six weeks.
- Establishing a significant automation infrastructure that will eventually enable Continuous Integration (CI) and continuous delivery (CD).

Stage two – Building new products/platforms

- MD (Multi diagnostics/devices) – a software product that would leverage the diagnostic engine – which until now had provided a solution for only one phone at a time – to a solution that provides a response for up to 40 phones at the same time. The solution would allow entry into a completely new market – the AMS market.
- Software as a Service (SaaS) – a user-friendly solution which would facilitate all company services through a cloud service, resolve the implementation problem, and allow extensive customer use by retail chains of all types and sizes. In addition, the construction of generic back office tools for all license and customization issues, which would make it unnecessary to tailor solutions to specific customers.

- Mobile Application Platform - a solution that would facilitate all our company's services through mobile applications, without the need for physical connection by a cable to a computer.

Third stage - Big Data:

A large database that would serve as an artificial intelligence infrastructure, primarily intended for a variety of forecasting capabilities for smartphones such as predicting malfunctions, performance, behavior, and more.

The technological revolution

The technological revolution was expressed through several aspects:

- Modeling the layers by building micro-services that enable robustness and quick addition of new functions (scale up).
- Eliminating the need for a phone warehouse for creating phone's database, thanks to Smart Crawler rapid search software that brings all the data that are relevant to a particular phone from the Internet, online.
- Rapid transfer of data between two phones using WiFi direct.
- A variety of patents in the world of diagnostics, such as:
  - Identifying the battery's condition using machine learning (completion of a patent already in process).
  - Distinguishing between hardware and software faults by transferring the phone to safe mode.
  - Troubleshooting the device by isolating modules and components.

    o   Identifying a broken screen by a remote software solution and machine learning.

The SaaS and mobile platforms are presented in a layered architecture by Figure 3.

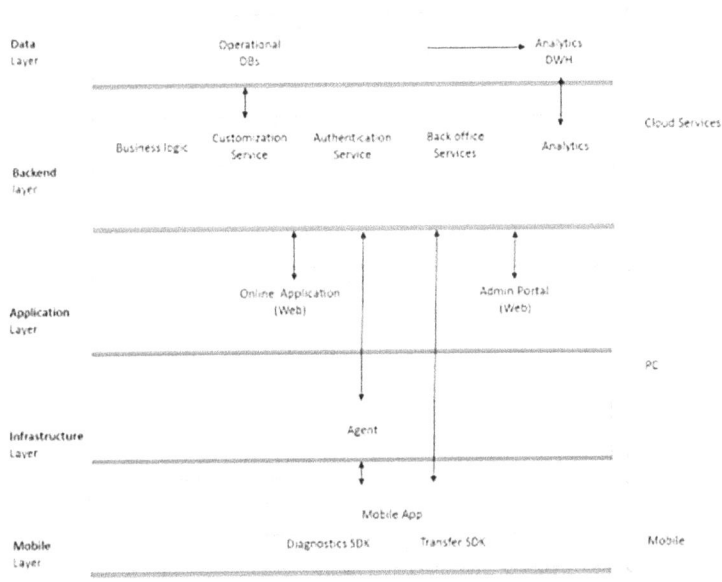

Figure 3 – Architecture of the mobile and SaaS platforms

The organizational change

As mentioned, we approached the second stage in realizing the strategy, i.e., the development of four different product lines, as described in Figure 4 below:

- Continued development and maintenance of the hardware products.
- Development of a new SaaS platform.
- Development of a new platform for mobile applications.

- Development of a Multiple Diagnostic Devices (MD) product for the AMS market.

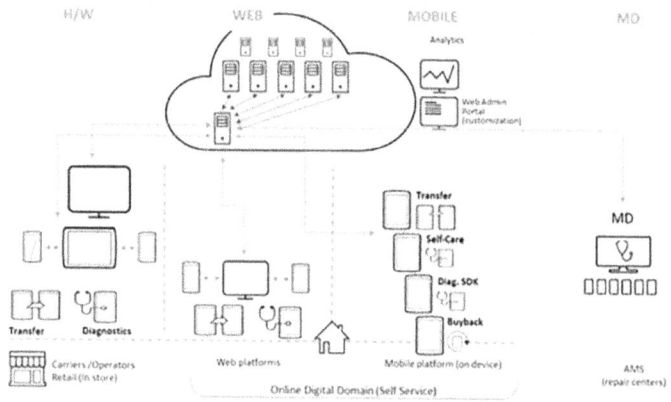

Figure 4 – parallel development of four products

The challenge was to develop four different product lines simultaneously. Up to this point, the whole organization focused on one product line – hardware-based products only, and in regard to organizational structure (as described in Figure 5) we operated in a configuration in which the R&D teams were divided into professional groups, and only the Release Manager was responsible for releasing new versions to customers.

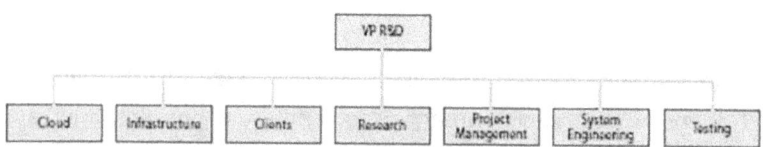

Figure 5 – functional/professional organizational structure

Of course, such a structure cannot grow into such an aggressive parallel development, and we were required to organize differently.

Our R&D management examined the issue from several aspects, including meeting with several industry leaders, to try to understand how they were organized to face similar challenges. The guiding principles we set for ourselves were:

1. Timely compliance with schedules, while maintaining the quality of our products.

2. Prevention of bottlenecks – simultaneous, parallel development without reciprocity and without dependence between the various projects.

3. Each group that develops a given product line must have the capacity for end-to-end delivery, and all capabilities and tools needed to perform the task (self-contained).

4. Technological depth must not be harmed as a result of an aggressive timetable.

The need to develop in parallel and independently, while maintaining quality and professional expertise, led us, during the first half of 2017, to establish a structure of "guilds and gangs" (as described in Figure 6) as follows:

Professional guilds (professional responsibility):

♦ Professional expertise (such as Android, iOS, QA, full stack, etc.).

♦ Architecture, code review, planning.

♦ 'How' – how to develop.

Gangs (responsibility for performance and delivery):

♦ 'What' we deliver – content.

♦ 'When' we deliver – end-to-end responsibility for the relevant product line, with total capacity for mission performance available (all types of development functions, QA, etc.).

- Quality of delivery.
- Plans and auditing.

A detailed explanation of the structure

1. Each professional (guild) group manager accepts responsibility for a gang (in addition to the group), which requires team managers to leap from the level of group managers to the level of overall development managers including delivery, and to cooperate with each other in distributing resources, and day-to-day activity, between the gangs.
2. A Product Manager was attached to each Gang Manager/ Development Manager. The pair bore joint responsibility; the Product Manager was responsible for the business angle and for the "what," and the Development Manager was in charge of performance and execution.
3. The team leaders filled the professional function of guild leaders, and provided a professional, broad response to problems discovered in the teams, across all the gangs.
4. The development resources were clearly marked; it was made clear who is in which gang.
5. Almost all developers and testers also sat in gangs. Anyone who completed a gang mission and received permission from his gang manager, could return to their guild and carry out general infrastructure works that benefited all gangs.
6. The lateral functions that were left outside the gangs and provided services to all the gangs were: System Engineering, Project Management, DevOps, Research, Automation, and regression testing.

Group Names	Guilds Skill Set	In store Platform	Online Platform	Mobile Apps	MD
	Management	x	x	x	x
Client	Android		x	x	
	IOS		x	x	x
	Web App		x		
Infrastructure	On Prem Core	x	x		x
	On Prem App	x			x
Cloud	DBA/Data Analytics Architect		x		
	Cloud Core	x	x	x	x
	Cloud Mgmt.		x	x	x
	DevOPs				
QA Prog.	QA MD				x
	QA In Store	x			
	QA Mobile			x	
	QA Online		x		
QA Reg.	System Level Testing	x	x	x	x
	System Eng.	x	x	x	x
	Research				
	Release Mgmt.	x	x	x	x

Figure 6 – matrix structure of Guilds and Gangs

The organization change in the R&D organization created an R&R change in the entire organization, as described in Figure 7, and positively affected the overall company, a fact that enabled delivery and deployment at a level different from what was customary before.

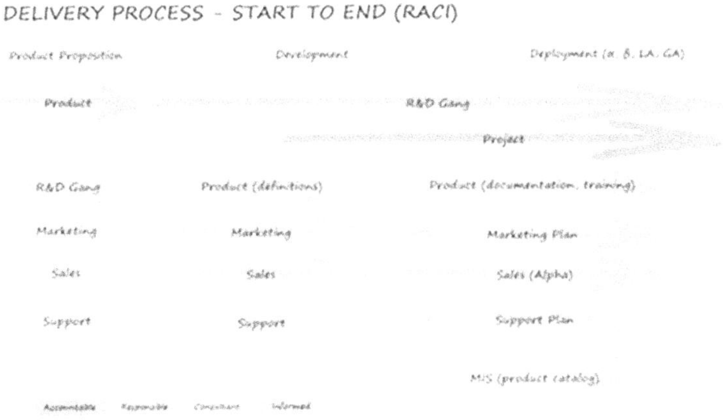

DELIVERY PROCESS - START TO END (RACI)

Product Proposition	Development	Deployment (α, β, LA, GA)
Product		R&D Gang
		Project
R&D Gang	Product (definitions)	Product (documentation, training)
Marketing	Marketing	Marketing Plan
Sales	Sales	Sales (Alpha)
Support	Support	Support Plan
		MIS (product catalog)

Accountable Responsible Consultant Informed

Figure 7 – R&R among all organizational functions in the course of the developmental process

Conclusions in retrospect

1. The entire process, from the diagnosis stage to execution, including the necessary organizational change, was orderly and correct.
2. Combining testing and development into one unit, which made it possible to make a joint decision to move towards a structural change, proved itself to be correct.
3. The harnessing of the product to Gangs proved to be correct; this made quick decision-making possible without the need for dependence on anything beyond the Gang.
4. The organizational change was a dramatic turning point in the quality and speed of releasing products by development. If we had been wise enough to do so earlier, we might have reached the market with the SaaS and mobiles platforms sooner, which would have affected the entire market.

The brand-building plan

The subject of brand-building was one of the first issues I brought up when I joined the company, because all the indications I received during the first few weeks at work were that our brand was 'carrying a negative charge' at that time.

Before proceeding, it's important to consider the definitions and features related to 'brand':

What is a brand?

For our purposes, I shortened the definition as it appears in Wikipedia:

> *A brand is a marketing term that describes a company, a product, or a product line. The brand term refers to the sum of all existing attitudes, emotions, and perceptions of consumers regarding the object. These attitudes and feelings are sometimes also called "brand assets." The goal of the marketer is to attribute values to the brand, such as quality, prestige, pleasure, or good value for money. However, consumers definitely may have negative attitudes toward a particular brand. This will usually be considered a failure of the marketing process.*

From this we can understand the subject's importance – a positive value for a brand is worth money, and it's important to be more positive compared to the values of brands that directly compete with it.

Brand value is worth money that can come from two main sources:

1. It's possible to charge a higher price for it compared to a similar product with a lower brand value.

2. Its market share can be expanded (more sales) at a lower marginal cost than a similar product with a lower brand value.

How to build a brand

There are several parameters that must be addressed in building a product and how they are related to our plan:

1. **Focus** - What features do we want to attribute to the company? The greater the focus, the greater the chances of success in building a brand with a high positive value. We decided to focus our brand-building on technological innovation. However, technological innovation for its own sake is insufficient; you have to make sure that it generates real positive value for your customers. For example, if our product will enable to generate higher revenue to our customers than a similar product based on less advanced technology, that's real value.

   Another example: if the innovative technology enables the seller in the store to complete a certain action faster, the profit is twofold:

   (a) The customer is more satisfied, because they can continue their way sooner.

   (b) The store owner is more satisfied, because they can handle a larger number of customers with the same personnel.

For this purpose, we formed a team that included marketing, product, and R&D leaders. The goal of this team was to identify, within the framework of work programs that were being formulated, the capabilities and features that could be defined as 'technological breakthroughs with real value to the customer' that we could advertise in intervals between three and six months. The intention was to produce marketing hype every few months about our releasing a certain capability that will connect to our positioning purpose – that we're a company of leading technological innovation.

The first capability that we identified was the ability to "clone" (replicate) cellphone content; i.e. the ability, when buying a new phone, to move all existing information on the old phone to the new one, so everything on the new phone looks like the old one did. This is a technology that didn't exist then, and was designated for completion by the end of 2016.

2. **Consistency** – To continue what was stated in the last paragraph, we set up a well-defined group to meet on a regular basis, once a month, to ensure long-term consistency. A single activity that supports building the brand as planned is just the beginning; we need continuity of many years to establish the brand, and later to deepen and even expand it, so that the name of our company – that is, the first connotation connected to our company's name – would be constructive technological innovation.

3. **Brand promotion** must be based on recommendations by existing customers. Advertising supports and preserves the brand, but it isn't enough in itself. So, when you come out with a new product or feature, part of any arrangement you make with the first customers should include using them as brand promoters. There are a variety of ways to do this. For example:

- Ask the customer to write a case study or to produce a video, which includes information about a new product or feature of yours that they have adopted, and how it helps them. You can also offer to produce the video for them; that is, the company pays for and takes care of production, but the video is associated with the customer and speaks in the customer's name. We did this several times, and it worked very well.

- Ask a customer to make a presentation at a professional conference, which describes in detail how they adopted your new feature and how it helped them. Alternately, an easier option is to invite a customer to make a presentation at a professional conference in collaboration with your company.

- Invite a customer who has adopted the product or feature to give a presentation at the company customer conference.

- Produce a joint press release of the customer and the company.

- Ask the customer to allow you to use them as a recommendation to other customers.

- Ask the customer to post about the new product or feature on social networks such as LinkedIn, Facebook and others, and in relevant forums and professional groups.

- Expose information about the feature (preferably shortly before the product is launched) to analysts or opinion leaders in the field. Of course, everything has to be done according to the facts on the ground; if there is already a satisfied customer, you can give more information to the opinion leader about how the new feature is actually used, and how it helped the customer, and suggest that the opinion leader contact the customer.

4. **Advertising** – advertising preserves the brand's resilience after its birth. You have to invest in targeted advertising after brand exposure, and we did make limited and focused investments in advertising, especially in relevant professional forums.

5. **'Protecting the Environment'** - An innovative new product or feature, however important, won't survive as a positive brand without preserving high-quality 'environmental conditions.' What do we mean? An innovative technological product which includes problematic issues such as:
   - Bugs that interfere with product operation.
   - Version update challenges.
   - a faulty user interface that makes it difficult to operate the product.
   - Poor customer support and more, cannot remain a positive brand.

   Therefore, brand-building cannot be a goal in and of itself; it has to be part of a series of goals and targets that the organization sets for itself. We'll elaborate on this point in the next chapter.

6. **Name association** – what do you build your brand name around? Many books have been written on this topic, and indeed there are several options. Let's concentrate on two:
   - Building the brand around the company name. We do this to strengthen and focus the company name, so that it's also included in the product's name. A prominent example of this method is 'Boeing' (any Boeing product also bears the company's name). Some automobile manufacturers use this approach, and many other companies do as well.
   - Another approach is to build the brand name around a product or around a new product line. There is considerable difficulty here, because splitting resources by constructing two brands or "expanding the brand" isn't recommended.

The result of this approach – which can be positive as long as the company plans it properly – will be that the product's name is what will define the company, and not the company's name.

In our case, we had to build a long process that included first creating a new name for the company (because we're a spin-off), followed by incorporating the names of our product lines under the company name. That is, canceling the current names of the products, and converting them to a name that will include the new company's name.

An important note – because we were a spin-off from a larger company which was well-established in its field, with a very positive brand name, we decided, at the first stage, to leverage the company's existing brand name and include it in small letters under the name of the new company we created.

7. **Name, logo, and color** – we'll highlight a number of decisions we made:

    ♦ Name – this must represent our own domain and uniqueness, and that's just what we did. The name was a combination of mobility, information, and science.

    ♦ Logo – we decided that the logo would include elements that represent our specialty. The logo included a graphical design of three squares, which represented replication of cellphones.

    ♦ Color - We chose a combination of the following colors:
        ◦ Turquoise – which represents communication and clarity.
        ◦ Blue – which represents trust, responsibility, honesty, and loyalty.
        ◦ Green – the color of environment and health.

Of course, you have to be consistent, and use of the selected colors in all the brand's marketing channels.

8. **Geographical focus** – In practice, a brand has no boundaries. For all the reasons which we have noted so far, we focused on the United States and Western Europe. However, during the world's largest exhibition in the cellular field in Barcelona, which took place later, dozens of potential customers from regions we hadn't previously focused on approached us, demonstrating that there are no boundaries to a brand.

The process of building the components of our brand: company name, logo, colors and more, was done with the full cooperation of the employees.

In practice, suggestions of a name for the new company came from our employees, after we set criteria to define a name. At the end of the name-selection process, the employee who suggested the name won the company appreciation.

Creating a new name for the activity also means creating a new identity in the consciousness of employees, suppliers, and customers.

It's important to note that right up until the launch of all the brand's components, things were done as part of a positive and constructive experience by all organization's parts. Fear and doubt set in only a moment before the launch, at the last moment before the employees had to disconnect from a name which had served the company's business activity for 17 years.

The moment of transition was filled with more than a few concerns, including those of the company's employees, but also of the administration about how customers and suppliers would take this change. For the employees, the fear was about a loss of stability, about separating from something that had proven itself a stable anchor for many years.

We prepared in advance a messaging list that would define us as an organization under the new name, as part of the larger brand-building program that included technological focus and leadership, which would enable us to create products that provide the broadest and highest-quality response to our customers' needs.

Despite the concern, and the pressure of several managers to delay the launch date of the name and all that accompanied it, we decided not to change the launch date, which included a new name, logo, email address, and a website focused only on our activity. In the second half of 2017, all the indicators we received from the field indicated that the process of creating a brand as we had planned – began. The process itself will last for years.

But the most important indicator was that at the beginning of 2018, we could raise prices according to the plan we had set up, thus significantly improving the profitability of the products that we sold, while also increasing market share, even though our products were more expensive than competing solutions. These were the first signs of success of a program that had begun 18 months earlier.

Defining annual targets and building the annual budget

The two tasks of defining targets and building an annual budget define the heart of the organization's activity.

There are two stages to this:

- Setting targets before the beginning of the year.
- Monitoring performance, and adjustment of the budget under special circumstances.

The two tasks are intertwined. One cannot be completed without the other.

Defining annual targets

In all the organizations I worked in, the definition of annual targets was an integral part of the budget-building process, and was defined by the executive management team.

This document had two main objectives:

1. To enable deriving from it the targets of each department and each employee in the organization.
2. At the end of the year, it defines the organization's 'grade' – the extent to which the targets were met – down to the grade of each individual. A combination of the organization's grade and individual's grade will define the financial conditions per

employee for the following year. If an organization has a bonus budget, these grades define the bonus for each employee.

How do you build such a process?

The process should be derived from the company's vision, which defines the organization's activities over a number of years, and will include the components which management has designated as targets for the coming year.

There are three main stages in such a process:

1. Defining targets in detail.
2. Defining the weight of each target, so that the total weight of all targets is 100%.

   You can go one step further and add a positive coefficient in the case of meeting the target, or a negative one in case of significant non-compliance.
3. Verifying that targets match the organization's budget plan.

Defining targets in detail

This depends, of course, on every organization, but I will mention the main issues that were important to us, and how to build focused targets:

1. **Financial targets** – Many parameters can be included here; I will note some of the most common:
   - Annual Revenue greater than $X. Depending on the organization's needs, a more complex target may be defined, such as: revenue by quarter (as defined in the "profit and loss" target), or median revenue, or other indices.

- Operating profitability and/or EBITDA (profit before interest, taxes, depreciation, and amortization).

- Gross profit margin - the difference between sales revenue and cost of sales is gross profit. The gross profit margin is the ratio in percentage between sales revenue and its direct costs.

- There are times when it is important for us to encourage the organization to sell a product because it is new, or particularly profitable, or for any other reason. In this case, one of the parameters can be, for example, revenue from the specific product or number of orders of the specific product.

   We must be aware, however, that orders have no financial value. For example, if we received an order for a three-year subscription software license for three million dollars, from an accounting point of view we will recognize one million dollars in the first year, while the remaining two million are order backlogs, which we can convert into revenues only over the following two years.

- Working capital – defined as current assets (financial values presented in the company's balance sheet, including all of the assets that can be converted into cash in the near future, usually up to a year, minus current liabilities. Total current assets versus total current liabilities allows us to understand to what extent the company is liquid. Financial liquidity is a measure of the company's ability to repay its debts on maturity. Financial liquidity is usually expressed as a percentage of current liabilities.

- Cash flow is an important parameter, and if we define it as a target, our payment terms and our collection system must be very tightly controlled.

- Raising money, in case the company needs external funding in order to realize its growth plans.

Who is responsible for meeting financial targets? – the entire executive team. There isn't a single factor that has no impact on the organization's compliance with financial objectives: sales, marketing, finance, development, quality, product management, information systems, human resources and others.

2. **Products** - Here too there is a long list of parameters which can be measured, each company according to its condition and goals. The following can be included as targets:

    - The list of products the company plans to complete this year. You can define what 'complete' is – if you mean the alpha testing level, a trial with customers (beta), or complete completion (GA - General Availability). Of course, one can add due dates as well as part of the target.

    - Successful completion of pilots, i.e., testing a product with a customer, which will meet all the requirements the customer defined before the trial begins.

    Usually, the target is the number of pilots, or the specific customers for whom there is a desire to complete a successful pilot.

    - Market penetration by a new product. This can be encouraged by including the monetary value of a product's sales as a target. There is another way of course – to motivate salespeople. We must remember that salespeople want to sell to get commissions, so they concentrate on selling what is easiest for them. One way to encourage them to sell new products is to give them a higher commission for the new products, and if needed, we can limit the higher commission rates for a given period of time.

Who is responsible for meeting product targets? – this depends on the industry sector and on the company's structure. In start-up companies, the responsibility for meeting these targets will fall on development, product management, quality, marketing, and sales.

3. **Customers:** The type of company, products, and customers will define the relevant targets. Some examples we used were:
   - Increasing the use of the product by a specified percentage, in reference to a list of pre-defined customers.
   - Holding a quarterly strategic meeting (QBR - Quarterly Business Review) with designated customers.
   - Holding CEO meetings to share information and market directions with pre-defined customers.
   - Improving the annual customer survey by X points. If a previous customer survey wasn't done, doing one can be defined as a target.

Who is responsible for meeting customer-related targets?

For this type of targets, the responsible groups are sales, product management, marketing, R&D, and QA.

4. **Internal processes** – this can include a wide variety of topics if you don't want to make a separate category for each of them. Examples of such targets are:
   - Defining R&R (role and responsibility) matrix for the organization.
   - Defining the product release process, and following up on its execution.
   - Selecting an external eCommerce engine, and connecting it to the organization's information systems infrastructure.

- Improving the accuracy of existing information on CRM (Customer Relationship Management), after defining accuracy indices.
- Meeting a pre-defined target for the number of faulty units per product during a product's first year.

Who is responsible for meeting targets related to internal processes?

Because this category contains a variety of targets, usually the responsibility will be matched to the specific target.

5. **Employee development** - maintaining high levels of mutual commitment between the employees and the organization.
    - Excellence in recruitment (based on pre-defined parameters).
    - The grade on a survey of the company's employees – higher than X or an improvement of Y points compared to the survey from the previous year.
    - Reducing the turnover rate below X%. (Turnover can be calculated as the percentage of all employees who left, whether at the employees' initiative at that of the company, or only the percentage of employees who left at their own initiative).
    - The turnover rate of key employees = 0%.

Who are key employees? These are employees whose capabilities have significantly higher impact on the company performance than others. In other words, the contribution of each of them to the organization's success is significantly greater than the contribution of the other employees.

Each department manager must submit a list of such employees, which must be approved by the CEO, human resources and finance; a plan should be built for each key employee, according to their needs. This can be a professional or managerial development program and/or a special compensation program contingent on their remaining in the organization over time and, of course, on their job performance.

Who is responsible for meeting these targets? – Management as a whole.

6. **Calculating the weight of the targets** - this depends very much on the type of company and at what stage in its life cycle it is.

If a company generates revenue, in most case, the financial targets will carry a significant weight, since unless the organization's financial targets are met, the other activities and goals are in danger. Therefore, the weight attributed to this area should be at least 50%.

The weight of the other targets is highly dependent on the organization's focus for the upcoming year.

The following is an example of targets:

	Corporate Goals	Owner		Objectives	Weight	Zero	200%	Total Weight %
Financial	Achieve strong topline growth	All	1.1	Total revenue >$xxM	15%	< 75%	> 125%	50%
			1.2	NON-GAAP EBITDA – profit to be at least $X or Y%	20%	< $X	> 1.5X	
			1.3	Growth engines (To be clearly defined) should comprise more than 20% of yearly revenue	15%	Less than 10%	> 30%	
Products - Sales Execution Targets + Roadmap	Develop the Market and Diversify the Revenue Mix	PdM, R&D, QA, Sales, Marketing	2.1	Meeting the roadmap Deliver 100% of critical roadmap on time and with requisite quality (based on GA process) 2.1.1 Product A 2.1.2 Product B 2.1.3 Product C	10% (evenly split)			24%
			2.2	Complete successful pilots 2.2.1 Complete minimum 8 pilots in H1 with product A 2.2.2 Complete minimum 4 pilots, at least 2 in H1 with product B	2% 2%			
			2.3	Penetrate market – customer deal goals 2.3.1 Close Product A deals with more than 20 customers, where at least 8 are from EMEA/APAC and at least 8 are from the Americas (min $50K/deal) 2.3.2 Close more than 10 deals with Product B, where at least 4 are from EMEA/APAC and at least 4 are from the America (min $50K/deal)	10%	Less than 50%	Up to 200%	
Customer	Improve Customer Engagement	PdM, R&D, QA, Sales	3.1	3.1.1 Increase overall number of Transactions performed, compare to last year 3.1.2 Increasing usage within 3 customers using current Product C 3.1.3 At least one business review with all Tier 1 customers 3.1.4 Improve overall customer survey score compare to last year	10%			10.0%
Internal	Successful Execution of High Quality Product Releases, including Optimized Go-To-Market Launches and Roll-Outs	All	4.1	4.1.1 Sessions success completion rate > 90% for products A & B starting Q2 4.1.2 Marketing to establish 3 new online campaigns for features/products 4.1.3 Define digital domain uptime/downtime (using industry best practices) by end of January 2018 and meet targets 2.1.4 Establish ecommerce & achieving more than $XX in sales	10%	Less than 80%	More than 95%	10.0%
Growth & Development	Maintain High Levels of Employee Engagement	All	5.1	5.1.1 Managers to demonstrate high standards of excellence in the recruitment (based on defined SLA) 5.1.2 Maintain engagement survey score X and above 5.1.3 Decrease Turnover Rate to be under X % 5.1.4 Turnover rate of Key employees = 0%	6%			6%

Building an annual budget

There are several philosophies regarding how to build an annual budget, but I will only address the way we built ours, with the focus on the process and questions which we had to pay attention to. It is important to emphasize I am describing a standard process similar to that of other companies, at least in the companies where I worked. I will also emphasize in what ways our budget-building process was slightly different from the standard one.

There are two pillars to budget-building: expected revenue and expected expenditures.

Building revenue projections

The revenue forecast is typically constructed bottom-up in the following stages:

1. What do we sell? – according to the company's work plan, it is known which products or services will be sold, and what their price will be, during the upcoming budget year. This is the basis for starting work on building projections. All the new products' details must be entered first into the organization's CRM, through which sales personnel can enter the data.

2. Who defines the sales forecast for next year? This depends very much on the company, the type of products or services, and sales channels.

   Whom does this include?

   - All direct sales personnel. Those who manage customers directly.
   - Sales channel managers. Sales channels can include:
     - Distributors.
     - Affiliates (if sales are online) and online sales manager.
     - OEM (Original Equipment Manufacturers) – companies that sell – as part of their product or as a complementary product – another manufacturer's product, usually under their own name (private label).
     - Inside sales managers (sales vis phone calls only).

3. **How do you define the sales projection?** Each forecaster will record, for each one of their customers or distributors, what they expect from them in terms of products, quantities, timing and probability level. If there is a forecast to start working with new customers or adding new channels – all these will be included in the program.

4. **Senior sales manager's forecast supervision** – Forecast supervision isn't simple, and complex variables enter the picture, for example:

    - Historical accuracy of each salesperson.

    - Distribution of purchase orders per salesperson – in the case of a salesperson responsible for a channel or customer whose purchases constitute a significant share of the company's total revenue forecast (generally above 10%), we should be much more conservative in our estimate.

    - Is this a new or old product? You should always expect surprises with new products, such as a major bug that causes the product to crash, which means stopping use for a period of time and making a refund for that period, or, if it is a hardware product, returns may be higher than expected.

    Another possible problem with a new product is not being accepted as compliant with the standards requirements of a particular country when the time comes.

    There are many other reasons for being conservative in revenue projections for new products. Therefore, experience in setting the projected sales probability of customers and channels sales is worth a lot.

5. **Financial supervision** - At this stage the data will be transferred to the CFO or to an analyst, to conduct statistical tests to verify compliance with a long list of variables. The goal is to test the

probability level of realizing the projection, given historical variables as well as market variables, such as taxation in different countries, exchange rates, and more.

6. **Completing construction of revenue projections** - after several interactions between sales personnel, through sales managers and finance personnel, the final forecast will be formulated. Because we have also taken care to add the projection of revenue by time period, we can see the projected income levels by months and quarters.

7. **Direct expenses – COGS (Cost of Goods Sold)** – This is the seam line between the company's revenue forecast and the expense forecast, related to cost of sale (direct cost of what the company sells). These costs include parameters such as:

   ♦ If this is a hardware product – its cost (materials, assembly, final testing, inventory, compliance with standards, deliveries, etc.).

   ♦ If this is a software product – data storage costs, data streaming, servers, DevOps, etc.

   ♦ Customer support.

Gross profit margin

The difference between sales revenue and cost of sale is the gross profit, and the gross profit margin is the ratio in percentage of profit to revenue.

This is one of the most important parameters, because it defines how much money actually remained in the company to operate its various activities.

Just to give a sense of this topic – let's say a company sells products for $50 million a year, and that the cost of the sales is

$30 million. This means that its gross profit is $20 million and the gross profit margin is 20/50 = 40%. If we succeed in increasing the gross margin by improving the production process that will allow reducing costs, increase the use of automated testing, etc., and if these activities can reduce the cost of sales from $30 million to $25 million, that is, an improvement in the gross profit margin from 40% to 50%, an additional $5 million will remain in our hands, which is a 25% improvement over the original gross profit ($20 million). This can radically change the company. From personal experience, such an improvement is achievable, but only if the organization's senior management comes up with an overall plan to achieve this.

If the gross profit margin is such an important parameter, why isn't it included in the above table as part of the organization's targets?

As noted at the beginning of this chapter, each organization has its own target focus.

The example given in the table represents a company that is making a move from selling hardware products to selling software and applications; that is, the company is focusing on launching as soon as possible the new platforms, where the gross profit margin is over 80%, meaning an improvement of tens of percentage points compared to the gross profit margin on the hardware platforms. Therefore, during the first year in which the software products are supposed to come out, a difference of a few percent in gross profit, however important, remains of secondary importance compared to the timing of the product's release to the market. In this specific case, moving up time-to-market by a month is worth a lot more in the overall financial calculation than an improvement by a number of percentage points in the gross profit margin; therefore, it wasn't included in the targets.

It's important to emphasize that in the past, when I ran a company in which majority of product lines were hardware-based, increasing gross profit rate was always included as a target of the organization.

Continuing to build the budget

Concurrently with the process of constructing the sales forecast, each VP was requested to build their department's budget. In order not to build budgets detached from reality, the CFO gave an initial assessment of the budget range for each department.

There was not one case that the budgets submitted were unchanged (in general, they were reduced). It seems that managers anticipated a cut, and therefore submitted a relatively large budget, assuming that even after the cut in their budget, will still allow them to meet their targets.

After we already had an estimate of the sales and gross profit forecast, we were free to go through their budget with every VP, which included a discussion about the necessary adjustments while avoiding harm to the department's ability to meet its targets, which are derived from the targets of the organization.

The overall process lasted two months.

The beginning-of-the-first-year crisis

The 2017 budget was approved a month before the end of 2016. Then, in the course of two months, the last month of 2016 and the first month of 2017, were on a roller coaster.

As we have already mentioned and will elaborate on later, we decided to build our brand around technological innovation. As part of the process, a short period of time after the formulation of management (four months earlier), we defined a plan that included developing technologies that were part of the product roadmap for the next two years, and which would serve as tie-breakers in regards to the products that existed at that time in the market, putting us in a leadership position.

The first development, as mentioned in the chapter "The brand-building plan", was the ability to "clone" phones, that is, to transfer, with unmatched speed, all the contents of one phone to another, so that it is impossible to distinguish between the original phone and the new one. Both features, cloning and speed, gave us a significant market advantage. Despite the fact that two manufacturers of the world's leading phones also had such a solution for their products, we could perform this function between two phones of the same manufacturer and more importantly, between two phones of any two different manufacturers as well, and our solution was much faster.

We launched this solution at the end of 2016, and thanks to that, we signed the largest agreement the company ever made, close to $10 million, with one of the world's largest cellular operators. The agreement was signed on December 31, 2016, an amazing finish to a year.

However, two weeks later, there was a sharp plunge in mood due to the revelations described in this chapter.

During the first two weeks of January 2017, six months after we started the process and shortly after the budget was approved, three serious issues fell upon us that created a big hole both in our budget and in our development.

A fiscal hole

It turns out that in North America, there was a lack of coordination between the regional sales manager and the CFO, and the projection of purchase orders timing was incorrect. While according to the plan, most of the P.O's should have been received in the first half of 2017, in practice they were expected to arrive only in the second half of the year.

Why was the timing difference of a few months so significant?

We'll demonstrate with the following example: if a license order at an annual rate of $3million is accepted at the beginning of January, all three million dollars would be recorded as revenue for that budget year. If, on the other hand, the same order is accepted in December, of the three million, only one month's worth can be recognized for that fiscal year; that is, only $0.25 million is recognized in the current budget year, and the other $2.75 million is recognized as revenue in the following year, so actually a deviation of 11 months from the beginning of the year produces a $2.75 million deficit in the budget for that year.

In our case, there were different numbers (from the above example) that accumulated to a significant sum. The error actually cost us more than just the deviation that was created, because in this budget year (2017), most of our sales were still based on hardware infrastructure. We made sure of hardware availability for the first half of the year, and an average shift of six months added to our hardware financing expenses.

How do you close such a gap? In fact, the fiscal gap couldn't be bridged unless we canceled our aggressive plans to develop new product lines, but we couldn't give that up. We all agreed that without these plans the company has no future; that is to say, without the new developments we couldn't reach a balanced budget the following year (2018).

In order to compensate for part of the gap, we decided to stop recruiting several new functions, mainly in sales in North America.

Unexpected development

1. The R&D plan for the following 18 months included preparing infrastructure to enter the AMS world by developing a software product (SaaS) to test 40 phones at once. We had once started developing a similar product but didn't finish it then, and we assumed we could continue and complete this project in a few months. This assumption turned out to be erroneous. The code infrastructure was faulty, and we arrived at the conclusion that there was no choice but to rewrite the code almost entirely from scratch.

   This has created a problem for us on two levels:

   a. We would have to allocate resources to develop the new product beyond what we had planned, which would harm development times on other projects.

b. We had expected revenues for this product already this year (2017), and postponing the launch required us to reduce the current revenue forecast.

3. At the beginning of the year, we found that we had to tighten the protection system of the data we accumulated as part of the data flow through our system. This was mainly in regard to protecting old information, due to complicated scenarios that some of the customers asked us to be able to handle. Because this was a demand that could have delayed orders if we didn't fulfill it, and also because of the forecast that data regulation (GDPR) would be tightened, which indeed came into effect later, in May, 2018, we decided to address this matter immediately, and to leverage it further on in the framework of our advantage in data retention.

The problem was that even though we shifted most of our development resources to this project, this development still took a whole month, which created a gap of one month in all our development plans.

The significance of this gap was that apparently we wouldn't be able to launch our new platforms at the General Availability (GA) level at the end of the year (2017), but only early the following year (2018), which would also contribute to the budget gap created in 2017.

The unexpected assignment

Less than a year after I began working at the company, during the first half of 2017, I was called to a meeting with the Board of Directors, and given an assignment to sell the business on its behalf. The sales process should end before the end of March 2018.

As I mentioned in the introduction, the essence of splitting business units into separate companies allows each business activity to focus on itself only, and at the end of the process, one or both activities are usually sold.

I was surprised, not by the mandate for the sale, but by the timing. When I got this job, it was clear to me (even though I had never been told explicitly) that the organization I was hired to manage would be sold. I estimated that this would happen within three or four years, so I would have a year and a half to make the change that will produce initial results after a year, and after three years, we would see impressive results.

The challenge to sell the company at this point in time was great. From past experience, it was clear to me that I couldn't involve other members of the senior management at this early stage. We must remember that we had a young and new management team, all focused on the creation of a revolution in the company, and to move them out of focus at this moment would be devastating; the managers might concentrate on the sale, and neglect their day-to-day work.

Therefore, I decided to take a step-by-step approach:

1. To concentrate on ending the quarter successfully – we still had a month and a half left.
2. To prepare an initial plan for approval by the Board of Directors.
3. To bring the CFO into the picture in early July, and to carry out the project with his help.
4. To delay including other members of the executive management in the project for as long as possible, until we reached the point where we need their help, and then to add them to the process as necessary.

The question that immediately disturbed me was how information leakage would affect the sale. Of course, if the news reached our competitors, they would make good use of it (to our disadvantage). It should be remembered that even though we presented ourselves as a separate business activity, from a legal point of view, we were still part of a large and well-established company which was considered high-quality and stable. Our customers were large customers from the retail world, and in this environment, stability is very important, while uncertainty and instability – and specifically about the identity of who may purchase us and how this would affect the quality of our service – might prevent us from winning big tenders.

Another cause for concern was the fact that it is quite possible that the process would not succeed. We must remember that the company was in the midst of a turnaround process, and the actual results were supposed to appear only at the beginning of the following year. That is to say, the sale might not be carried out, in which case we certainly would not want the information that we tried to sell the company to leak out.

This sensitivity to confidentiality also had to be taken into account when we had to decide which type of company to turn to – should we focus on strategic buyers or financial buyers? We'll present more about this in the following chapters.

However, although most active steps would be taken only later, it was important for me to use the limited time left until the end of the quarter for high-level planning of the process and raising the main issues which must be dealt with:

- Building a schedule that includes the main milestones.
- Main messages – Value proposition.
- What is the target price?
- Defining critical employees – those required for the success of the process and will be required to invest considerable effort. Also, how will we reimburse them for their very significant effort?
- Selection of a financial consulting firm that specializes in managing such a process and representing the company being sold (sell side).
- Preparing contingency responses if employees or customers ask questions about the sales process, due to leakage of information.

It is important to emphasize: it was clear to me that the company must continue with its business plans and all targets as defined by the management.

The master plan

The goal was to create an initial plan to make sure it would be possible to comply with the timetable, on the assumption that the organization's work plans must not be harmed, and that at the first stage there is no intention to involve additional management members except for the CFO.

1. Building **a timetable** that includes the main milestones, which are:

    ♦ Procedural issues, such as defining critical employees for the process, preparing contingency answers, and defining the main messages.

    ♦ Within three months – selecting an investment house and signing a contract with it.

    ♦ Within two months of signing the agreement with an investment house – a series of meetings with candidates for the purchase.

    ♦ Within three additional months, i.e. eight months in total – an agreement with the leading buyer, which would leave us two months to negotiate and sign a contract.

2. **Definition of critical employees** – those required for the success of the process, who would be required to invest considerable effort. Also, how will we reimburse them for their very significant effort?

    At this point all members in our executive management would be included, and given three roles:

    ♦ Participation in the sales process, including meetings, presentations, conference calls, etc.

    ♦ Continuation of regular work in order to meet all the defined targets for the business activity that they were responsible for, and the company's goals in general, during this important year.

    ♦ Management of crises that may appear as we progress with the sales process, whether vis-à-vis employees, or customers and partners, and crisis management immediately after the sale, if happens.

In conjunction with the board of directors, we determined a compensation sum for managers. The sum for each manager was different, depending on the influence of each member of management on the sales process, and the size of the team they manage.

3. **Selection of an investment house** – that is, a financial consulting firm that specializes in managing a process of this type, that represents the selling company (sell side). An orderly selection process would begin at the end of the quarter, after the CFO would become involved. We will discuss the process in detail in the next chapter.

4. **Preparation of contingency responses in case employees or customers ask questions due to leakage of information** – I formulated one answer to a question, which from past experience would be the only question that would be asked. The answer that was formulated was the best one that could be given, and it also accurately represented the actual situation.

Question: Is the company in the process of being sold?

Answer: There will always be those who will try to buy companies of our size that are operating in a growing market like ours. This has happened in the past with our company, and it will happen more in the future. Every time we get an offer, it is transferred to the Board of Directors, that decides whether to accept it or not. There were already such offers in the past which were turned down.

The sales process

Towards the end of the second quarter of 2017, I updated Ido Tzur, our CFO, about the sales process.

We defined the following tasks:

1. Formulation of initial thinking on the type of purchaser we were looking for.
2. Finding an investment house.
3. Preparing for the construction of data rooms.

The next chapter, which describes these tasks in detail, was written together with Ido Tzur.

Before we proceed to describe the process, it's important to understand the basic difference between the two main forms of selling a business activity:

Selling a business activity through an "Asset Sale" or a "Stock Sale"

The business activity we are talking about was not yet a separate legal entity, even though it was functioning independently with its own separate budget.

Asset Sale

In the framework of an asset sale, an incorporated legal entity sells its operational activity, or one of them, to the acquiring legal entity. In a transaction of this type, all of the assets and liabilities (both tangible and intangible) of that operational activity are usually sold.

An asset sale will usually include:

1. The intellectual property (IP) of the company's products: patents and trademarks.
2. Contracts with customers and distributors.
3. Asset balances: customers, and accounts receivable and payable, related to the activity being sold.

In addition, in the context of an asset sale, a demand may arise to convert contracts with employees and suppliers to the acquiring company.

Since an asset sale takes place on the operational activity level and doesn't directly deal with the level of the company's shareholders, in general, customers, employees, and suppliers will have to approve conversion of contracts they signed with the selling company to new contracts with the acquiring company or agree to assign them to the acquirer.

In an asset sale, statutory liabilities vis-à-vis various governmental authorities usually remain those of the seller. For example, obligations to pay taxes on income, if required in the future by the tax authorities, will usually apply to the seller.

It should be noted that when a company executes an asset sale of only some of its business activities, such as the sale of one business division within a corporation with multiple divisions, then there is a need to identify and separate the assets and infrastructure that support the operations of that specific division, before the sale. Examples of a recommended separation:

1. Web sites.
2. Configuration and software code management systems.

3. Separation of cloud infrastructures.
4. Customer accounts, suppliers, etc.
5. Development infrastructure.
6. Marketing infrastructures.

Stock Sale

In a stock sale, the corporation's shareholders sell their holdings in the company or companies that comprise the business activity. This kind of sale is possible when the assets of the business activity being sold are incorporated in a separate legal entity (or a number of entities).

A stock sale includes all tangible and intangible assets owned by the company that is being sold. In a sale of this kind, the buyer is usually also given statutory obligations vis-à-vis the tax authorities and other authorities.

In the framework of a stock sale, agreements for the conversion of contracts aren't usually required of customers, employees, and suppliers, since sales of this type change the company's ownership structure, but not the legal structure of the company itself, and therefore, there is no need to convert contracts. However, significant contracts with customers and suppliers may include various stipulations which continue to apply in the event that control of the company is sold.

Considerations, in the framework of the sale of a business, in selecting between an asset sale and a stock sale

When a business activity is sold, both the buyer and the seller have a variety of operational, legal and tax issues to consider.

When the corporation's sole activity is sold, after which no business activity will remain in the corporation, tax issues will usually have the greatest effect on the decision: **an assets sale creates a tax liability on the selling company, whereas a stock sale creates tax liability on the shareholders of the company sold.** These issues are complex, and this book won't enter into examining them.

When only one of the selling corporation's activities is sold, beyond taxation issues, additional operational considerations appear, which we'll focus on later. We'll also analyze the main considerations from the seller's point of view.

The seller's considerations in selling a business activity: an asset sale or a stock sale

Asset Sale

Advantages of an asset sale	Disadvantages of an asset sale
Immediacy: There is no need to establish a separate legal entity before the sale.	Uncertainty as to whether the transaction will indeed be realized, since it may be contingent on the assignments of contracts with the company's main customers and its employees.
Cost savings: The seller isn't required to invest resources in splitting the company before the sale.	Pre-sale operating limitations: If a number of business activities exist under one legal framework in the pre-sale situation, operational complexities may arise. Examples include joint signature rights, lack of flexibility in information systems to support various activities, policy and expense structure which doesn't match the needs of the activity being sold, and so forth.
	Difficulty in identifying the assets being sold, and difficulty in the separation of shared infrastructures, are liable to make it difficult to transfer the activity, both in the due diligence stages and in the stages of transferring the activity to the purchaser (transition).
	The seller usually remains with commitments and statutory exposures in respect to the activity being sold, such as the need to file tax returns and to undergo reviews of them in the future.

Stock sale

Advantages of a stock sale	Disadvantages of a stock sale
Total sale of the activity, including statutory obligations and exposure to tax and other authorities.	Assuming that the activity being sold wasn't incorporated as a separate company, it's necessary to make a pre-sale legal split. This split may be a long and expensive process for the seller, that will be executed before the sale is even certain. The split process may include the establishment of separate information systems infrastructures and conversion of contracts with customers, suppliers, and employees, all at the seller's expense.
Identifying the assets and liabilities of the activity which is being sold in the separate company/ies.	Splitting a company before its sale may produce tax liabilities, even if the activity isn't sold. Although according to local law (depending on the country) there may be measures to defer tax until the sale of the activity, the implementation of those means may impose limitations on the splitting companies.
May avoid the need to convert contracts with customers, employees and suppliers (most likely not fully, depending on the structure the contracts).	

Splitting companies – company divestiture or carve out – is complex in a wide range of operational and legal aspects, as well as in regard to taxation. There are many considerations regarding the separation of legal entities of the activity being sold, that can simplify the sale process. However, the legal split that the seller must carry out is a complex and expensive process, whose feasibility isn't necessarily clear to the seller before it has found a buyer and before the sale, and many sellers may prefer to leave the "headache" to the time of sale and perform an asset sale in this case.

In this context, advance planning of the legal structure in line with the business structure is probably the right answer. When there are several business activities in one corporation, and there is a likelihood that sooner or later it will be necessary to make structural changes, either by an outright sale or by the introduction of investors into any activities, their separation in advance into different legal entities may be the right holding structure. Legal splitting at a later date, at a stage when a plan for the sale of an activity is already in progress, may not be practical. As they say, look ahead.

Who are the potential buyers?

There are basically two types of potential buyers:
- Strategic purchasers.
- Financial purchasers.

Strategic purchasers

The varied potential strategic purchasers for any company can be divided into two main groups:

1. **Competitors** - competitors who operate in the same field, who have clear motivations to purchase a competitor: increasing market share, strengthening market status, cost savings and more. It is very important to understand their motive, which can be one of the following:
    - Acquiring better technology that they lack.
    - Expanding market share through additional customers, new sectors, or additional distribution channels.
    - Expanding geographic activity, entry into new geographical markets.
    - Expanding their product portfolio.

However, experience is the best teacher, and I can testify that in most of the meetings that I had with competitors in previous acquisition discussions, their real motivation was to pump information out of us, or to obtain assistance in negotiations held in parallel with the aim of acquiring a third competitor. Therefore, there is sensitivity to disclosing information to competitors, even if it is all done under confidentiality agreements.

In M&A discussions in this case, the other party will be overly sensitive to confidentiality in the course of the negotiations, since they understand the risk that exists if the company they are interested in acquiring is sold in the end to another party (another competitor or a new entity in the market), which may put their position in the market at risk.

A point to think about – before we entered this orderly sales process, a connection was created through a third party with a large competitor with a significantly broader activity than ours in regards to selling our company. After a brief series of meetings, they decided not to continue the discussions. Two months later, in a meeting with a strategic customer of ours, the customer noted that they had heard from that company that we were seeking to be acquired. This is a classic example of how just the mere knowledge of our intention to sell could be used to our disadvantage.

When selling a company to a competing entity, there is a potential for obtaining a high price, but equally – if not more – there is a high risk of breach of confidentiality in a way that could cause damage.

2. **Acquirers from complementary markets**

These are companies that operate in close/complementary markets, and the acquisition of our company would allow them to expand, and strengthen their market positioning.

In our case, potential buyers of this kind could have been

insurance companies or companies that purchase second-hand phones and are looking for a way to create a presence in stores which we do.

In discussions with purchasers of this type, the level of risk of leaking or misuse of information is lower than in discussions with competitors who are potential buyers.

A deal with strategic buyers usually takes longer in comparison to financial buyers, and the process is even longer when it comes to a potential buyer from a complementary market, since there is a learning process, and after that, a financial analysis process that will affect the value that the buyer is willing to pay for the company. All this takes time.

Financial acquirers

Financial purchasers, or investment funds, are entities whose main business is the acquisition, improvement, and sale of companies in the medium term (several years).

The financial buyer's main objective is amelioration (financial improvement), i.e., the acquisition of a company for a certain amount, the improvement of the activity, and then its sale for a high sum).

Investment funds are prepared to perform a variety of types of transactions, starting with the acquisition of 100% of the shares, through the purchase of shares from only some of the shareholders, through performing the deal in several stages, while the shareholders remain in the company until its sale for a high price to a strategic buyer.

The risk level for violation of confidentiality in contacts with financial entities is lowest, since strict confidentiality is in their interest, and part of their DNA.

The most common types of financial purchasers are private equity funds, which are funds established to make investments. Such funds are managed by a Fund Manager, who may be a private person or a designated company which was established for this purpose. Usually, this is a businessman, or a group of businessmen, that raises capital from various entities, such as pension funds, insurance companies, banks, and particularly wealthy private investors, who are legally considered limited partners.

Investors are committed to injecting sums of money into the private investment fund which will form the basis of its investment activity. The fund starts by locating investments according to a pre-agreed policy, and acts to realize them at the end of a period which was allotted to it in advance.

A pre-agreed policy will include parameters such as:

- A specific field of activity: retail, technological, medical, etc.
- Companies up to or of a certain size (value, income, or profitability).
- A defined geographic location.
- Other parameters.

A private investment fund has an expiration date when it ceases to exist – for the most part about 10 years, with the possibility of extension for several more years. Often the Fund Manager will continue their role and recruit a new fund that will continue its predecessor.

The private investment funds industry began operating in the 1960s, in the United States. Since then it has spread to other countries, and today there are thousands of funds that manage investments in hundreds of billions of dollars.

A decision regarding the type of purchaser

Given the information discussed:

- Length of the process (longer with strategic purchasers).
- Risk of information leakage (high with strategic buyers).
- Price (high with strategic buyers).

and given the directive to end the process before the end of March 2018, we decided to concentrate on financial buyers, despite the expectation that a price from such entities would be lower.

Another important point was taken into account – as already emphasized, a financial acquirer or private equity entities whose main activity is purchasing companies, improving them, and then selling them in the medium-term time period - In our special situation, there was a strong synergy with financial acquirer goals, because all our activities were intended, in the first stage, to reach a budgetary balance, and immediately afterward to expand the company's business activity, a fact that was intended to increase its value within a few years, so it would be likely that a situation of resale within a relatively short period of time would be created.

In other words, the idea was that being acquired by a financial institution would allow us to continue operating in our current format while improving the company, until it was sold again in a few years.

Finding an investment house

Due to the short time for the process and the complexity of the sale, (an asset sale, not a stock sale) and since, in addition, Ido and I were busy over our heads in managing the company's ongoing activity, I decided to take an investment house which would in effect manage the process.

To select the investment house that is right for us, we defined the main parameters by which we would evaluate the various candidates:

1. A company based in the U.S., but which has a history of locating buyers around the world.
2. A company that represented the seller in most of its sales.
3. Average sales value of less than $200 million.
4. A high success rate in closing transactions.

Together, we located five companies, and we had a series of phone conversations with each of them.

The companies' analysis of our business unit was similar; they identified the following characteristics in us:

1. Leading technology that serves Tier1 customers.
2. A significant market share.
3. A company on a growth track.
4. A company which is undergoing a transition from a hardware platform to a Software solution as a Service (SaaS), but still at the very early stage of the transition, and there aren't concrete positive results yet.
5. A company looking for an asset sale, with all its complexity.

We decided to focus on the three companies that best matched the parameters that we had defined. One company's headquarters was in Seattle, the second was in New York, and the third was in Boston.

Immediately after the end of the quarter, Ido and I went out for three days of meetings, a company a day.

After weighing all the data, we have decided to go with the company from Boston.

The process of signing the contract with them was quick. The only point that delayed it, and which is worth referring to, is that we in no way agreed to link paying them a fee for the sale to future investments, or the sale of any of the mother company's shares.

Moreover, all the proposals we received from the three companies were similar in structure; almost their entire proposed fee was dependent on the success of the sale, with only a very small part being a monthly recurring payment for a limited period of several months.

In August we had a signed contract, and during the next month, we went deep into the process of preparing materials and setting up a data room.

In parallel to preparing the material for distribution, the investment house sent us a long list of financial institutions who might be potential buyers. We requested to approve each company that would be sent details about the sale.

The process of approaching potential acquirers

There were several phases in this process.

1. **Do you wish to receive information?** – in the first step, a one-page executive summary (which included general information with the project code, without the company name) was sent to potential acquirers, to which a confidentiality agreement was attached.
2. **Granting access to Phase1 information** – the company name was revealed to companies that signed a confidentiality

agreement, and they received access to the data room, where basic documents on the company were found. Of course, we could see all the transactions in the data room, including who examined each document.

3. **Deciding on a meeting** – a three-week period was defined within which potential buyers had to decide if they are interested in a face-to-face meeting, whose date was set up in advance.

4. **The meeting stage** – a meeting at this stage will take one to two hours.

The meetings were concentrated in four main cities in the USA, and everything was performed in one week.

After this week, companies had a three-week period to decide if they are interested in issuing an IOI (Indication of Interest) showing their seriousness about continuing the process.

It is important to emphasize that the offer in the IOI wasn't binding, but only those who made one advanced to the next stage.

We prepared for the meetings in the course of a day and a half in Boston. The preparations phase was a very important step in which we practiced our presentation of our offer to sell before the investment house's internal team, and we could examine in real-time every message and every emphasis in our presentation. It was very important to us to be precise in details and to deliver the message that we so deeply believed in about the dramatic change that our organization was going through.

In this kind of preparation, a team of analysts also sat with us, so that if we decided to expand the information about the size of the market or a change in a segment of the market in recent years, there were people present who knew how to produce this information almost immediately.

5. **A letter of seriousness** – IOI (Indication of Interest) The next step after the initial meetings was accepting non-binding proposals. We received five proposals, from which we chose to continue with three investment funds, whose proposals were within our expectations.

   As soon as we received the offers, it was time to update the management team about the sale. This I did in personal individual meetings that included explaining and sharing full information about the entire process, starting with the Board of Directors' decision and providing details of where we were in the process and what the next steps would be.

   Every one's reactions were similar: a combination of "Why now? Why can't we wait another year to see results from the significant moves that we made?", and Interest in the sales process that from this moment on, they became full partners in.

6. **In-depth meetings** – one step before the end included adding more detailed information to the data room and face-to-face meeting with each of the investment funds, with the executive management broadly represented.

   Each meeting lasted between a half a day and a day, during which we presented the breadth of the company's technological, commercial and business activities.

   The three funds were given a period of time to submit an LOI – a Letter of Intent.

7. **Selecting a candidate for purchase:** If we receive an "LOI – Letter of Intent" from more than one company, we must choose only one company, and then move on to an exclusive due diligence process with that company (we mustn't negotiate at the same time with other companies) after which a purchase agreement should be signed. We wondered: will that happen?

At this point, of the three investment funds, there was one that we connected to, both in regard to its business concept and in regard to its management, and a second one that we didn't know how to digest. It was a fund that carried out many acquisitions, but it was difficult to get information about how it functioned.

As mentioned, three funds were given a certain time period to submit an LOI – Letter of Intent. According to the original plan we were supposed to allocate a month for submission of the letter, but we decided to prolong it a little.

We were close to the end of 2017, and it was important to us that all the acquisition candidates would have updated data for that year, and we could publish that data only at the beginning of 2018.

2017 was the last year the hardware platform was designed to be the leading product. As discussed before, this platform had a very focused and limited market, mainly Tier1 customers – cellular companies' retail chains.

Relying on a relatively limited number of customers creates uncertainty in the ability to anticipate revenue. Delaying or bringing forward an order by several months significantly affects the income level, and since we were concerned that three potential customers would delay their orders by a few months, a fact that would harm the financial results of 2017, we wanted to make sure that the potential acquirers, received the updated numbers of revenue and profit/loss before the final decision, in order not to be dragged into a double negotiation: one before the final numbers of the year, and the second at the beginning of the next year, after we knew the numbers.

In practice, our concerns were realized, and movement of several projects by several months reduced our annual revenue level, and increased our concern on how that would affect the proposals for acquisition.

Preparations for setting up a data room

The data room includes all the documents needed for a company that is considering a purchase, in order to get an accurate picture of the company which is a candidate for acquisition.

I have included a representative list of documents required, so that you can evaluate the great effort and time needed to prepare all the material.

About the company

- A diagram of the legal structure of the company.
- An overview of the company on all subjects, such as sales, partners, investors.
- Board of Directors and all other relevant material.
- Detailed history and future data on the number of employees per department.
- An enterprise organization chart down to the department level, and detailed organization charts by functional groups (sales, marketing, support, etc.).
- Offices and factories according to countries and cities, including the employee count for each location.

Financial Analysis

- Detailed financial results for the past three years.
- Financial data according to customer types, license renewal, professional services, maintenance, support of sales channels, etc.

- Detailed analysis of recurring revenues, for the last three years, by customer size and by product.
- Key indices and values used to define the company's performance.
- Revenue from customers by type of income in the past three years (or the period available).
- Projections of revenue from those customers for the coming next year from new products and licenses renewal. Revenue by product, by type of income for the last three years (or the available period).

Market Size

- All estimates and calculations of the market size, including Total Available Market (TAM) and Serviceable Addressable Market (SAM).
- Market share calculations, and what is the trend?
- Competitive landscape and comparisons.
- New customers and customers the company lost every year during the last three years. To whom did we lose the customer, and why?
- Market studies (If there are) about market size and competitive landscape.

Marketing and Sales

- A list of our backlog of business opportunities for direct sale and through channels.
- Breakdown of all open orders by product type (hardware, licenses, services, etc.).

- Analysis of successes and failures against major competitors.
- Sales targets by salespeople and channels, compared to performance during the last three years.
- Order backlog, conversion percentage in the last three years. How do we calculate growth in order backlog?
- Sales strategy by customer types and markets.
- Case studies.

Products and technology

- Overview of the product portfolio and a description of our product release model.
- Product/technical architecture.
- Level of usability by product.
- Products roadmap.
- Description of hosting infrastructure, for example, company-owned data center, AWS, and so forth.
- A list of third-party products or licensed partnerships/software and open source dependency.
- Main intellectual property and patents.

Professional services and support

- Breakdown of services in the past three years.
- Pricing by service type.
- Marginal profit by service type.
- Analysis of services by recurrence: one-time or ongoing ("re-occurring").

- Backlog of regular services.
- A list of leading implementation partners in the past three years, and projected activity for the next year.

Historical and future financial information

- Detailed quarterly financial statements for the last three years (or available periods) and for the next three years, including main models and assumptions.
- Breakdown of operational expenses by department: Sales and marketing, research and development, general and administration.
- The last financial balance sheet.
- Actual performance vs. budget for the last three years.
- Capital expenditure (Capex) for the past three years (maintenance versus one-time expenses) and expected capital expenses for the next three years.
- In case we are speaking of a split of a company (spin-off): Timing of the split, shared manpower, shared infrastructure, etc.
- Details of plans for investing in R&D by product.
- Details of future investment plans.

Annual sales kickoff

Continuing our line of thought to continue the company's activities as if there were no sale process (something we actually executed), we gathered all sales personnel, product managers, R&D leaders and company management, for three concentrated days at the Dead Sea for the 2018 annual sales kickoff.

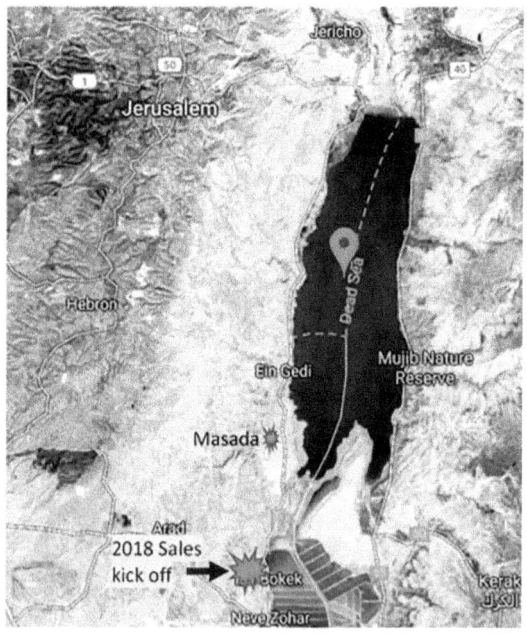

It is important to understand the complexity of the situation in regards to the sale of the company, mainly from the psychological aspect.

Along with the company's executive management, all of whose members were aware of the sale process at this point, we all felt that in this new year, 2018, the company has, at last, all the tools it needs to succeed. Given this background, to some extent we didn't want an acquisition offer to come, so we managed to disconnect from the sales process and focus on this important gathering, whose entire purpose was to make sure that, together with all our new products, this year was going to be a good year for our company.

The meeting's date was scheduled for the second week of January, at the Dead Sea. This venue was chosen for several reasons:

1. The Dead Sea is the lowest place on earth. As far as I'm concerned, this was symbolic – the company had reached rock-bottom, and from now on everything we've worked on to effect change would come to fruition and should show results. We could see that the financial indicators were all positive and rising, at the beginning of the year 2018, we already had a pipeline greater than all the revenue of the year that just ended, with a probability rate of over 75%, which means that I had all the indications that this year would be a breakthrough year.

2. The Dead Sea is a relatively isolated place, ensuring time for team formation, cohesion and solidarity. We had exceptional weather for the period of the year (the middle of the winter), which would allow recreational activities to promote employee cohesion.

3. It was very important that during the kickoff, everyone would be concentrated on understanding the new products, and on sharpening the company's overall strategy and the benefits it gives us. I think it's easier to achieve this goal in an isolated place.

4. A little different reason – personally, I feel different around sites with meaningful historical payload. When you're less than an hour's travel from Hebron, Jerusalem, Jericho, Masada, Sodom and Gomorrah, and the Qumran caves – it does something to you. As I told everyone in the opening session: "when you wander outside, keep in mind that you are stepping on endless footprints accumulated in this area over the last 4000 years."

The conference had four targets:

1. Team consolidation and cohesion– during the period I was in the organization, the sales team and employees with supporting functions never got together. I thought that exposing all the information planned for this conference would create vibes and positive energy, and it was important to produce some kind of positive feedback, in which everyone boosts everyone else. We also estimated that one of the outcomes of the sales kickoff, once the employees will hear and see the new products, the rate of employees leaving the company in 2018 would be very low, this was one of the drivers to invest and bring all our global sales teams to one place to form them into one unit. When our targets and goals for the year 2018 and beyond were clear to everyone, that itself would help us to achieve the goals.

2. Presenting the company's strategy, for the period from back in 2016 to the future of 2020. Although some things had been said over the past year in various settings, it was important to emphasize the change that our company is making, and how that would affect it in the following years:

   ♦ In the second half of 2016, we concentrated on the change of the DNA, the company's business strategy. We moved the center of gravity, the main energy of development, from adapting products to customers to building new product lines, which would include an option for each customer to adapt the product to its own needs.

- The year 2017 was used to build infrastructures to allow the company to expand its business, and this included:
  - New product lines, that we'll expand on below.
  - Our development method was modified from Waterfall to Scrum.
  - The QA testing was expanded to mass crowd testing – using testers located in different locations in the world, to enable testing our applications' performance on phones operating under cellular networks in our destination countries.
  - Automatic testing.
  - Changes in our entire customer support methodology. The new methodology was described, and so too were the results of the last few months. Not only were we able to keep costs steady, but we had a much more important achievement – the results were an order of magnitude better than at the beginning of 2017. We reached a 98-100% response to customers, in all languages. This subject, which previously was the company's Achilles heel, had become a company advantage, which we brought about by modifying the support group's structure, outsourcing support level1, upgrading support level2/3 teams, and using translators for several languages.

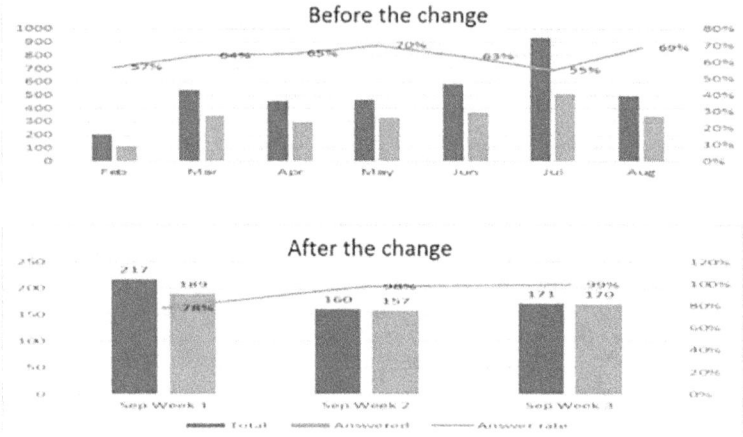

○ We established the Customer Success function, which proved to be a game-changer. On the one hand, for a year we could explore and understand what motivates some of our customers to use our products substantially more or less than others. In addition, we could leverage the insights we gained into consulting information that could be submitted to all customers, and could also improve our products during this period. These advances gave our company significantly greater value from our customers' viewpoint. One example out of many:

— In the framework of one of the first analyses we performed on the use of the diagnostics product, we've detected prominently high use by a certain customer in North America. On the basis of a series of questions that addressed to the customer, we received a detailed explanation of their business model. The customer forwarded us precise information regarding the level of savings it achieved when it avoided sending a repair phone to the manufacturers. To do so, it created a workflow whereby its shipping system prevented sending a product to repair that had not yet been tested first with our diagnostic product. The customer's updated workflow included a direct interface between its information systems and ours. The exact breakdown of this information was very helpful to us in formulating general recommendations to the other customers of our diagnostic product, which gained us a great deal of appreciation.

According to our plan, 2018 would be the most important year for our company, the year in which all the effort and changes made during the previous 18 months would be manifested.

Our new developments also came to the finish line, and at this sales kickoff, we revealed for the first time all that the R&D, QA and the product managers had been working so hard on for a whole year. To produce an amplifier effect, we also asked the R&D leaders to join us on the day we presented the new products.

The new portfolio included two separate product lines:
1. Expanding our current hardware-based product line to:
   - One software SaaS product, which allows business growth in several dimensions.
     - The same user experience that our current product provides inside the store to a limited number of large store networks (Tier1), the new product allows us to sell to any size of store chains (four times larger than the current Tier1 target market) due to its lower cost (but at a 30% greater profitability).

- It allows the large networks (Tier1) to expand their services to self-service as well, due to our new product's simple use.

- It will allow us to provide all customers with the same user experience, wherever a user needs to use the services, whether in the store, at home or on the move.

- It will allow us also to sell in online channels – so we also established a separate marketing group designed to produce the intended leads to small customers (Tier2/3) or to customers who want to purchase transaction packages and not a monthly or yearly license. For this purpose, we defined an eCommerce engine connected to the site, so that payments and issuing licenses would be performed automatically, including messages sent to customers before their license expires.

♦ Another product, that is actually an application, that allows the customer to perform most of the SaaS platform's capabilities. It was designed primarily for Tier1 customers, and will allow them to provide their customers with the same user experience wherever they are.

The amazing thing was that our new products were significantly better in all aspects of performance – speed, simplicity of use, and more – than those of the old system, and if you compare the number of lines of code, we are speaking about a few hundred thousand lines of code in the new system, compared to millions of lines of code in the original system.

2. The second system was targeting the AMS sector, which is very closely connected to the retail market. Here too we launched two product lines:

- A product that allows testing of 40 phones simultaneously, and knows how to do this in a fifth of time compared to the technologies and products of our competitors.

- A product that can be added to each of our platforms for testing the condition of a used phone which is intended for resale.

I highlighted the three phases we underwent in the last 18 months:

Phase One – changing our DNA, our business strategy, from a company that invests most of its energy to adapting a product to customer requirements, to a company that focuses on developing off-the-shelf products.

Phase two – launching new software application-based product lines, which will serve the entire overall cellphone market – both the retail and the AMS sectors.

Phase three – whose essence is the launching of disruptive technologies.

Our decision to develop breakthrough technologies had obvious goals. I see this as part of the company's strategy. That is to say, the very fact that the company comes up with a surprise every half year, something groundbreaking, whether in technology or in product, achieves a number of important goals which are part of the company's long-term strategy:

- Establish the organization brand itself as a leading creative company in ideas, technology, and products.

- Over time, such consistency produces customer expectations, so much so that customers, or potential customers, are avoiding adopting other solutions, if only because they're reluctant to remain lagging behind, with limited capabilities.

- A long-lasting creative position allows potential customers to justify to themselves paying higher prices compared to other products available on the market.

I adopted this strategy in the past, and it always worked. In the short term, it demands more investment in research and development, and therefore it requires a budget, but the investment returns itself over time, usually within three or four years.

During the last day of the sales kickoff, we revealed a new technology that we had been developing in secret for several months: with this application, we can diagnose whether the phone screen is broken or cracked. There still remained work to be done on this project, but we could already demonstrate a working prototype based on this disruptive technology.

The responses to our presentations were amazing; people were just standing there for ten minutes and clapping their hands, not only for the last demonstration, but for all they saw that was done in the last 18 months.

At the end of the sales kickoff, there was no salesperson who didn't contact me. I heard, again and again, sentences such as:

- "This was the best sales kickoff I ever attended."
- "It's clear to me now that this company is going to be a great success..."
- "This year, I'll exceed my sales target in a big way."

It was also important that the development and QA leaders were present at the conference on that concluding day. This was a big group of people who worked long hours every day for more than a year to get to the destination – to allow the company to embark on a new route.

At the end of the last day, I said goodbye to each of the participants and went up for a drink of coffee at the hotel's café. This was the first time in all this challenging period, mostly filled with hard decision-making and not-simple moments, that I could relax for one moment. Not only did we make a revolution, but we also got approval from the group, the salespeople, who must execute everything that we had planned and built. As far as I was concerned, it was confirmed the readiness of the organization, in all its departments, to embark on our new path.

But the momentary calm was interrupted a few minutes later. I checked my e-mails for the first time that day, and I saw two purchase proposals (LOI). Ironically, after the great success of the conference, if I had to choose a day on which I'd be glad if the sale didn't work out, that would be the day.

Boomerang

The entire process, from the distribution of the executive summary, to selecting a private equity firm, had lasted five months. An additional 45 days allowed a due diligence period and negotiating the purchase contract.

We received final offers from two companies.

Before entering the 45-day period, we invested time to check the companies, both private investment (private equity) funds from the United States.

The proposals were fundamentally different. If you are comparing cash payments at signature time, the offer from the Texas-based company was higher than the one of the company based in California. But the California company offered an additional significant sum, by using a conditional-value mechanism: earn out.

Earn out - a conditional-value mechanism

This mechanism states that part of the payable to the seller, is subject to the compliance of the acquired business activity with pre-agreed business objectives.

The acquirer's considerations in implementing such a mechanism are obvious. The acquirer will always prefer to reduce risks, to delay payment of part of the sale price, and make it more contingent on the acquired entity meeting business objectives within a defined time period. The acquiring fund knows that no matter how deep was their due diligence, there's always some information it's not aware of, and this information – whether the status of customers or competitors, issues related to intellectual property, and more – may possibly affect the future business results of the activity it acquired.

In such situations, the acquirer will search for ways to reduce risk, in order to ensure that the value it pays on the basis of past results will also pay off on the basis of future business results, in the period after closing the transaction.

Another significant benefit to the acquirer in the delay of payment is the advantage of cash flow – it's probably better for the buyer to postpone some of its payments for the acquired business, and to spread them over a few years. This reduces the cost of the primary financing required to make the deal, and also – and this may be the most important consideration – it allows the acquirer to finance some (or all) the payments by using the profit/cash generated by the acquired business.

Back to the two proposals. In a previous chapter on the sale, I mentioned a certain company with whom a good personal relationship between the executives had been created; this was a reference to the potential acquirer from California. Beyond the personal connection, even the business vision of our management and theirs, at least seemingly, was similar; that is, to concentrate on business growth after launching the new platforms, thus generating a significant revenue and profitability, in order to sell the company in another three to five years.

On the other hand, the company from Texas had an operational orientation, aimed at reducing operating expenses and focusing on operational profit. It wasn't easy to get Information about them, even though they were a company that had already acquired dozens of other companies. What we did learn as we kept inquiring them and companies they acquired, is that they intend to merge our activity into an existing platform, thereby releasing a substantial portion of our employees. Of course, the moment we found that out was a difficult one for us.

In light of the proposals, it was quite clear that the board would choose the company from Texas. If I were in their position, that would be my decision too, so I made clear to the company from California that without significant improvement in their offer, they would not win.

After many follow up conversations with the firm from California, they indeed made a better offer, but even that one was still less attractive in the cash aspect than that of the firm from Texas.

The day when we presented the alternatives to the board was a tense one.

The financial offers from both companies were clear and final.

The company from California's proposal wasn't as good as the other one, but they pledged to receive the company as is, including all employees and management.

On the other hand, the financial offer from the company from Texas, looking at the risk level, was better, but it was clear that the great majority our executive management would not continue, nor would a significant part of the employees.

As an additional alternative, we suggested to the board to postpone the sales process for 12 months, out of the belief that the upcoming year will be excellent for our company, and thus the company could be sold for an even higher price next year.

The proposal for a one-year postponement of the sale was not accepted, and since royalties from an earn-out proposal are always uncertain, the Board of Directors, taking into consideration all the information we presented them with, chose to proceed with the company in Texas.

Despite my disappointment and that of our executive management, we had to concede that the decision made was completely rational and reasonable.

However, the moment of the board's decision was a very difficult moment for us, the executive management. On the one hand, we were gratified that we had complied with the goal that was set for us, to successfully conclude the sales process by the end of the first quarter of the year. However, on the other hand, there was a feeling of missed opportunity, that we could have brought the company to an even higher level if we had been given the chance to continue on the path we had set out on.

From the moment the decision was made, all our executive management, with the support of the Board of Directors, focused on meticulously planning the day when the sale would be announced, with all that implied, including an alternate job at the parent company for those who would not be continuing in the acquiring company, and a severance package for those who would prefer neither to go over to our mother company, nor to continue with the acquiring company.

Notifying the employees

A week before Passover Eve, a few days before signing the purchase agreement, when the contract was all ready for signature, I gathered all our employees together for a toast for the upcoming holiday. It was important for me to connect between the approaching holiday of Passover and our, the company's executive management's, feelings.

The way I found to do so was through the story of Moses, and this is the essence of what I said:

It was the eve of the Passover holiday, and there's nothing like Moses that symbolizes this holiday for the Jewish people. Moses was a lone leader. While he was assisted by his elder brother as a spokesperson, he was the one who carried all the burden of the people on his back. On the one hand, Moses was a lonely figure, and on the other hand, he was a very powerful biblical character who changed the course of the history of the Jewish people. Without Moses, Israel would have remained a group of slaves to the king of the Nile river.

Let's start with the essence of the story – Moses grew up in Pharaoh's house, but at an unknown age (probably between 20 and 30) we unexpectedly learn that Moses was exposed, in surprising contrast to how his life was conducted up until then, to the suffering of his people.

At that time, Moses grew up and went out to his brothers, and then he saw an Egyptian hit a Hebrew man.

Moses, who seems to have been severely influenced by what he saw, decided to respond, and killed the Egyptian and buried his body in the sand. It turns out that his killing the Egyptian was discovered. Moses feared that Pharaoh will hear about it and have him killed, and thus he fled to Midian.

Before we talk about Midian, it is important to address Moses's mental state at this point in time. He feels great pressure in two directions. Firstly – someone who lived like a prince and was accustomed to being treated royally, and whom everyone listened to whatever he had to say, found himself more alone than ever, a fugitive on the run like a common criminal. Secondly– Moses did not feel that he belonged to any people. He ran away from the Egyptian ruling class he had belonged to all his life so far, and on the other hand, he felt alienated from the nation who was born into, but never really was a part of.

As the story is told, Moses escapes to Midian, a dry area in the northwest part of Arabian Peninsula which includes a large part of the eastern side of the Dead Sea. In Midian, according to the Scriptures, lived the descendants of a man himself named Midian, the sixth son of Abraham and his concubine Ketura.

Moses' sense of social justice, caring for others, that began when he helped that slave, which lead to the killing of the Egyptian attacker, continued upon his arrival in Midian – where he saw how the male shepherds drove the shepherd girls away from a well and prevented them from watering their flock of sheep. Moses intervened in their favor and enabled them to water their sheep. As a result, Moses was welcomed royally by their father Yitro (who is now revered as the spiritual founder and chief prophet of the Druze community) who gave him his daughter Zipporah as his wife. Two sons were born to Moses and Zipporah, Gershon and Eliezer.

Moses became a shepherd, for a period that lasted for several decades. At this time, he was far removed from all who were not his immediate family. He was alienated from both his Egyptian past, and from the Hebrew people.

At the end of this period, Moses experienced the vision of the burning bush, where God appeared to him for the first time and told him that he is the one who would save Israel from their misfortune. Moses sought to avoid this mission, but eventually, after much persuasion, he accepted it, and Aaron, his older brother, was appointed to serve as his spokesman, since Moses stuttered.

And now we come to the heart of the story.

And so, at the age of 80, Moses was sent by the order of God on the mission of his life – taking the Israelites out of Egypt and returning them to the land of Israel. Moses devoted forty years of his life to this task, a task that required infinite boldness and bravery.

And after he accomplished the leadership task came the most difficult moment as far as he was concerned: he wasn't allowed to enter the Promised Land.

Moses led the people during the 40 years of wandering in the desert. During that period, he was subject to many trials while leading the rebellious people, and he even performed many miracles. Yet at one point, he was punished, together with his brother Aaron, and was told that he would not be able to enter the Land of Israel.

And God said to Moses and Aaron: Since you did not believe in me, to sanctify me in the eyes of the children of Israel, therefore you will not bring this congregation to the land I gave them.

The Torah is vague about what brought about this punishment, but apparently, it was in the course of the incident at the place called Mei Meriva. When there was no water to be had, Moses and Aaron were supposed to speak to a rock, and miraculously, water would flow from it. Instead, Moses hit the rock. It is not clear exactly what Moses' sin was, but there are those who believe that he was deficient in his faith in God, and therefore struck the rock, and in the eyes of the people who were watching him, that act appeared to be a lack of trust in God. Thus it was that shortly afterwards, after all his tremendous efforts over 40 years, when he was just a step away from entering the Land of Israel, the land flowing with milk and honey, a stride away from the land promised to Abraham, Isaac, and Jacob, when he could actually see the Land from the Eivarim mountain and feel the wind blowing from it, God put up a divine wall between him and the entrance to Israel – "you cannot enter." Was there ever a more frustrating moment than this?

Moses did everything he was asked to do to bring the people of Israel to the Promised Land, he served the Creator for 40 years, and for some missteps which it is hard to believe were so weighty, he was prevented from enjoying the fruits of his hard labor. Moses did not give up easily, he simply pleaded:

And I pleaded with God at that time, saying: Lord God, You started to show your servant Your greatness and Your strong hand, for who else is mighty like You in the heavens and on earth; who can perform Your acts and has Your Strength? Let me pass, I beseech you, and I will see the good Land, on the other side of the Jordan River, the goodly mountain and Lebanon. And yet God was still angry with me because of you, the people of Israel.

There is no greater degree of spiritual humility than this. Moses went as low as one can; he did not conduct gradual negotiations, simply all of him became supplication. He expended infinite effort for 40 years on a mission he did not want, and now he arrived at the destination but was not allowed to touch it.

But Moses' pleas were not accepted, nothing helped. God interrupted him and gave him sharp and clear instructions:

But He did not listen to me. And the Lord said to me, That's enough! Do not speak to me anymore about this! Go up to the top of the mount, and lift your eyes south and north, east and west, and just look, because you will not cross the Jordan River. Give Joshua the command, and strengthen him, for he will cross, leading this people, and he will have them inherit the land that you see.

Moses would not enjoy the fruits of his great labor.

I ended the story with a relatively casual statement – I noted that, in my opinion, this is a difficult and seemingly unjust story, and in general, there are quite a few cases that seem to us lack justice, and still, we have to accept them and move on.

It was clear to me that many of the employees would see injustice in the move that was expected to be publicized in a few days, that despite all the hard and excellent work that had been done, they would not manage to benefit from its fruit.

A few days later, on the day the contract was signed, we gathered all the employees again to give them the message about the sale. Rumors at one level or another had been circulating for the previous few weeks, and after the meeting on the eve of the holiday, things did not come as a complete surprise.

It was important to explain the reason for what the management did, and to convey the message to the employees that we would take care of helping everyone to find their future, whether in the acquiring company or in a new place – and that's what happened.

Looking back

When all was over, I was asked quite a few questions by employees from all organization levels, from managers from the parent company to the last of the programmers. I think that the questions asked and the answers I gave are a proper summary of this book, so here are the questions and answers:

Q: How would you summarize the sales process?

A: Bittersweet. On the one hand, the target, the sale of the company within a pre-defined time period, was reached. On the other hand, we could have achieved a lot more if the sales process had taken place a year later, which would have enabled the company to continue to follow its long-term program. The immense gap between all the changes we made and the lack of time to see concrete results left a sour taste of disappointment.

Q: Are you sorry you took the job?

A: Definitely not. This job was an experience of productive activity and cooperation between management, the Board of Directors and employees, as well as an opportunity to bring about extraordinary change in a short period of time.

In an email sent by one of the employees, she included the following quotation:

"Don't cry because it's over, smile because it happened."
(These words were attributed to Theodore Geisel, who was better known as Dr. Seuss).

Q: Would you change the vision or strategy in retrospect?

A: No, I wouldn't change anything we did in these matters. Throughout the period, we challenged ourselves over and over again in regard to the direction and objectives that we set out for ourselves. As time passed, we received only positive confirmations of our decisions and the direction we went in.

Q: Was the BoD just trying to get rid of this business activity?

A: We must look at the picture as a whole – there are a variety of types of Board of Directors.

1. One type includes investment fund representatives whose every being is to invest in companies, with the goal that after a certain period of time, these companies will yield returns. The yield can come from distributing dividends from profits, or as a result of a stock issue by the company, or from its sale. The private equity from California was an example of this type of investment fund. It saw all the changes that had been made over the past two years, and identified a business opportunity in paying for the purchase of business activity according to past performance, and preserving the organization as is, in the belief that within three years, the changes made would have good business results, and it could sell the company for a big profit.

2. The other type, which is also common, represents our case in general. Our Board of Directors was made up of representatives

of two companies. The first company is the one that we were a business unit within. This company saw its future in business activities connected to the digital forensic market, and its management focused on improving the company's performance in this field, just as it should.

The owners of this company (and ours) served as Chairman of our Board of Directors. The owner company which by itself is an Asian vendor, also focused on improving its business activity.

To summarize this answer – the Board of Directors was assembled from the representatives of two product vendor companies, and each of the representatives' perspective was primarily focused on its own business activity, and only secondarily on us.

The very fact that we were a business activity which ran a deficit for several years, which they had to finance, impacted negatively the profitability and performance of each of the two companies, and once an attractive acquisition offer was received, they didn't hesitate to accept it, so that they could continue to focus on the growth of their main activity.

There is a professional concept that describes our status in the structure I described:

'a corporate orphan.' That means to say, our business activity didn't contribute to the focus of the board representatives, whose job was to care for the development of the companies that each of them led.

It's important to me to emphasize that if I were in their place, I'd do the exact same thing. That is, referring to the question as it was formulated, I wouldn't look at the sale from the perspective of "getting rid of" the property, but from the perspective of focusing on promoting a company's central business activity.

Q: In retrospect, should you have focused more on strategic buyers?

A: My experience in selling a company to strategic buyers in the past was that the end of the sales process, the price paid for the company was indeed high, and also the company remained in its original structure for the following few years. However, the length of the sales process was unpredictable or uncontrollable, because of a variety of reasons, most of which didn't depend on the company being sold.

In the case under discussion, meeting the deadline was significant, and defined the process. From the moment that this was the case, I still think the focus of selling to a private equity was correct. As noted, the essence of these financial funds is investing in or purchasing companies. These funds have an orderly acquisition process with a well-oiled mechanism designed to conclude such processes within a given time period, and they share it with the company for sale from the very beginning of the process, to ensure that there is coordination of expectations between the buyer and seller, and that was important to us.

Could we still have succeeded with a strategic purchaser? That's of course always possible, but I didn't think it would have been right to take such a risk, and I would do the same thing I did even today.

Q: Can a company really successfully make a two-dimensional business change in such a short period, launching new products as well as entering a new market (AMS)?

A: We must remember that when we created the business strategy that included, on the one hand, adding a Software as a Service (SaaS) product for the retail market, and on the other hand, entering the AMS market with a new product, we weren't looking at the range of a single year, but rather two years. The unexpected directive to sell the company came only later. If we had known at the time we determined our business strategy that we had only about a year to make the sale, without a doubt we would have put together a different strategy, but that wasn't the case.

The decision on the two-dimensional activity was from the expectation that these two markets (retail and AMS) will develop a strong mutual dependence, which will grow with the increase in second-hand phone sales, and in retrospect, that's exactly what happened. The significant orders we received at the end of 2017 were from retail chains that started working in the second-hand phones purchase/sale market.

Q: What was the purpose of the Board in splitting the business activities of the parent company, and did our activity match this goal?

A: The goal in splitting the company was to allow our business activity to reach budgetary balance as soon as possible, so that we wouldn't negatively affect the digital forensic activity's financial performance and the financial performance of the company that owned the two activities. Did our activity match this goal? I believe so, but there were things that, had we done otherwise, would have shortened the time need to reached budgetary balance. (See the following question.)

Q: Are there any basic things you would do differently?

A: Yes. I would change three essential things:

1. **Our activity in South America:** Immediately, at the beginning, it was clear to us that we wouldn't be able to sell extensively in South America, for all the reasons we mentioned earlier, until we released our new product lines. Indeed, I had great

respect our team in the area, but the real reason I didn't weigh closing our offices in South America was a contract signed with a Tier1 customer in the area, a number of months before I joined the company, which obligated us to remain active in this region. We shouldn't have signed that contract; it defined our commitment to sell, but not the customer's obligation to buy. In retrospect, I should have announced the cancellation of the agreement and closed our offices in the region. Even if we would have had to pay significant legal expenses in penalties for canceling the contract, we still would have saved millions of dollars each year.

2. **Our activity in Asia:** As I explained in previous chapters, the situation in Asia (not including Japan) was similar to the situation in South America. Unlike in Europe or North America, the great majority of Asian mobile users pay before use, not at the end of every month (prepaid rather than postpaid), and that has consequences for the sales of our products.

In most cases, in Asia the user acquires their phone from retail networks, but the cellular operator itself doesn't really have an incentive to sell phones, which it would want to do so only if that would tie the user to it. The business model of retailers who aren't cellular operators is entirely different. While the cellular operators are interested in the monthly payment for using the cellular network, and selling the phone is a tool to achieve this business advantage, the other retailers must earn on the sale itself, so they are very sensitive to the cost of the sale, which reduces the chance of our selling hardware-based products that have a relatively high cost. So although we did reduce our team there, in retrospect it would have been more correct to shut down our activities in Asia completely until the launch of our new software-based products.

3. **Splitting companies** – even though we intended to legally split the companies, we didn't get to that, and I think it was a mistake I didn't put on pressure to do so. Splitting the companies legally would also have brought about the above two beneficial actions, since we wouldn't have established legal entities in those areas. And maybe, and even more importantly, this would have allowed us to separate the CRM, IT, and ERP infrastructures. Doing that would have had two significant advantages: since we were a relatively small organization, our demands on these systems were more modest than those of our mother company's, so splitting would have reduced costs considerably, but more importantly – we could have then have made changes that would have matched these systems more closely to our needs, something it wasn't practical to do within one legal entity. It's obvious that splitting the companies could have had tax implications for our parent company, but nonetheless, from my narrow point of view, it would have been better for the split to have been carried out.

Q: Here's question that repeated itself many times – how much was the company sold for?

A: Tens of millions of dollars.

Summary

This period was undoubtedly a personal challenge for me, just as I had hoped. For all its complexity, we are speaking about a meaningful experience.

In such a situation, in which you try to make such an essential change in a short period of time, day-to-day constructive work with the executive layer who report to you on the one hand, and board members to whom you report on the other hand, is essential. I can say with a whole heart that it was a privilege to work with these two teams. In general, as managers, we depend on our subordinates no less than they depend on us, and there is no substitute for joint work based on trust, respect, and appreciation.

It was important for all of us, executive the managers and the board of directors, to take care of the employees, both those who continued with the acquiring company, and those (who were the majority) who did not. Our main concern was they leave well-prepared for the future, whether through an extended paid vacation or new place of employment. According to the responses I received in the last few months from dozens of employees, I believe that the vast majority enjoyed the period during which I managed the company, benefitted from the process I directed, and found a warm new place to work in.

www.ingramcontent.com/pod-product-compliance
Lightning Source LLC
Chambersburg PA
CBHW060825220526
45466CB00003B/983